TM

What Fish Eats What: A Few Simplified Fish Food Webs

A Combat-Fishing® Book
Written and Illustrated by
Bryce L. Meyer

Dedication: To all my biology teachers from grade school to grad school, who taught me how to see the forest AND the trees.

LCCN:2013900508
ISBN-13: 978-1481915595
ISBN-10: 1481915592

Best attempts were made to depict species and ecologies as known to science or my observations, but simplifications were required for the intended audience and possible unknowns. When in doubt refer to a scientifically accurate detailed source.

What is a food web?

A **food web** is a story of what eats what. Think of it like this, energy comes from the sun, is converted by plants or algae to more plants and algae, which are eaten by something, which is turn is eaten by something else. The result is the sun's energy moves down the food web as animals eat other animals. Food webs are just for a certain period in time and can change over time.

An example: apple trees use the sun to make apples, people eat apples, therefore sun energy moves from the sun, through the apple tree, to us. If we eat all the apples, there will be no more trees, so we eat something else, thus changing the Sun-Apple-People food web.

What do the arrows and pictures mean?

The pictures are symbols for a <u>population</u> of things. A **population** is a bunch of animals or plants of the same kind (**species**) that live in the same area, taken together. The arrows show what eats what. The head of the arrow points at what is doing the eating and away from what is being eaten. When something gets eaten its population decreases in number.

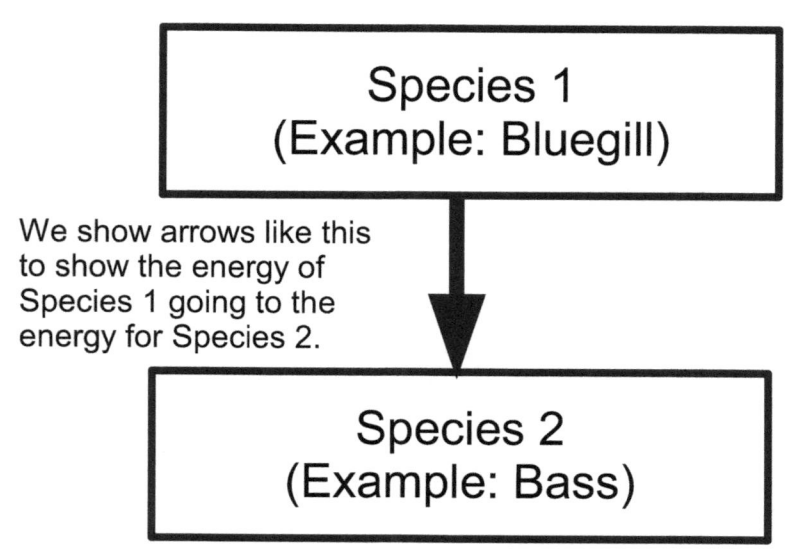

Species 1
(Example: Bluegill)

We show arrows like this to show the energy of Species 1 going to the energy for Species 2.

Species 2
(Example: Bass)

(Some of the population of) Species 2 eats (some of the population of) Species 1

Why draw a food web?

We draw food webs to try to answer questions. Since food webs are more complex than anyone can draw, we only draw the parts that help answer our questions.

Example:
QUESTION: How do people eating bass affect the bluegill population of a pond?

One possible ANSWER:
If you trace with your finger following the arrows you can figure out how something affects something else.

Bass eat Bluegill, People eat Bass. Therefore People eating Bass helps increase the number of Bluegill since it keeps the bass that are eaten by people from eating bluegill.

(Note: too many bluegill are not good for whatever they eat though, and if the bluegill eat too much they all go a bit hungry and stop growing.)

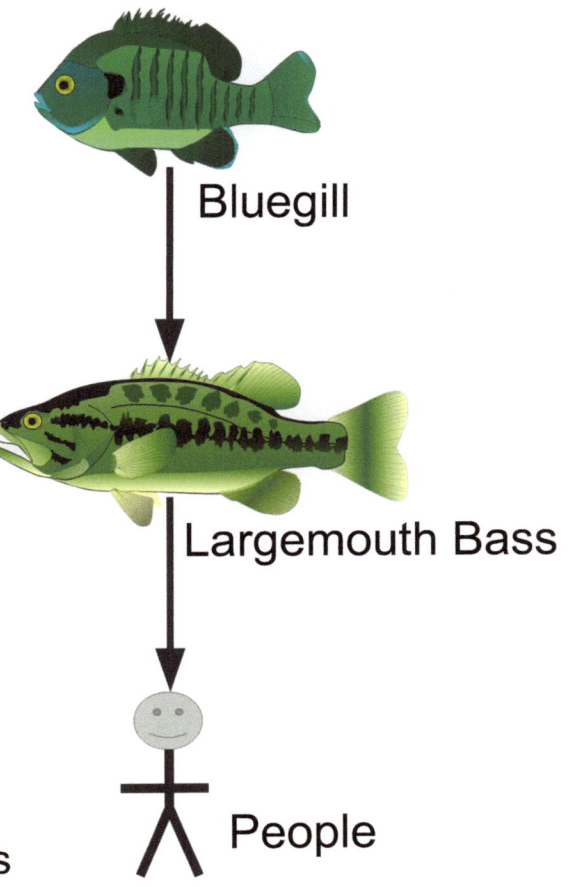

Bluegill

Largemouth Bass

People

WARNING: Even the best Food Web is not the whole picture of an ecosystem. You need other types of pictures too! An ecosystem is ALWAYS more complex then you, I, or anyone, can draw (In short: all the webs in this book are incomplete and best guesses)

Energy and Food

Energy goes from the sun (light) or from the Earth (heat, chemicals) to get converted into bacteria, plants, and plankton which get eaten by animals, which get eaten by bigger animals.

Plants, Algae, phytoplankton, cyanobacteria, convert Carbon Dioxide to Oxygen using light, everything else uses Oxygen and releases Carbon dioxide.

Sun

Nutrients, chemicals, from runoff, the bottom, etc

Bacteria, fungi, and Animals that eat dead Plants, animals

Plants, Cyanobacteria, and Algae And Phytoplankton

Larger Animals (including People) that eat Smaller Animals

Smaller Animals (including Zooplankton) that eat phytoplankton, bacteria, Algae, Plants

Hydrothermal Vents: Chemicals and Heat

Bacteria that convert heat and chemicals into energy

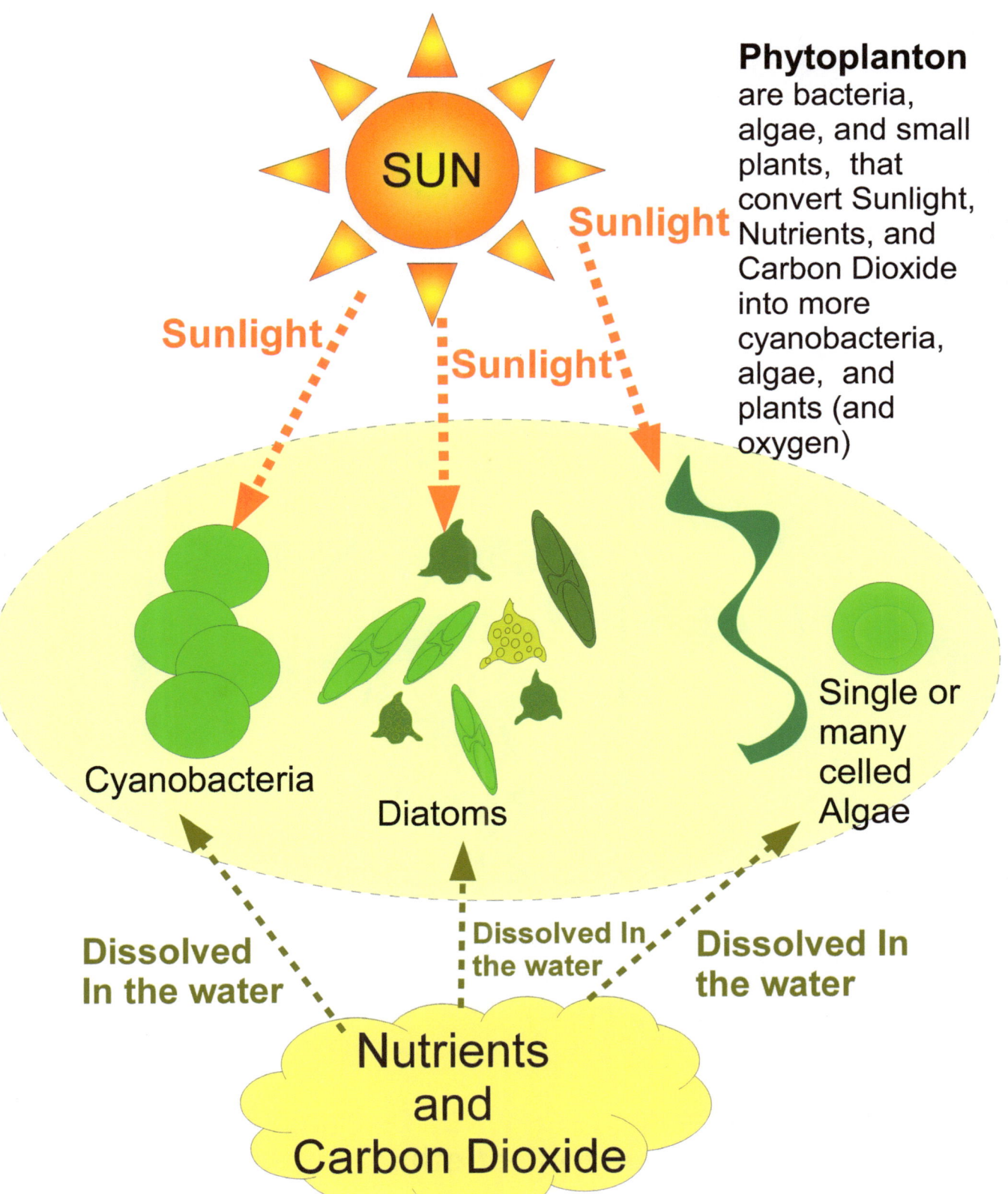

Phytoplanton are bacteria, algae, and small plants, that convert Sunlight, Nutrients, and Carbon Dioxide into more cyanobacteria, algae, and plants (and oxygen)

Phytoplankton in turn are eaten by many other things. They make sunlight into food for the rest of the food web.

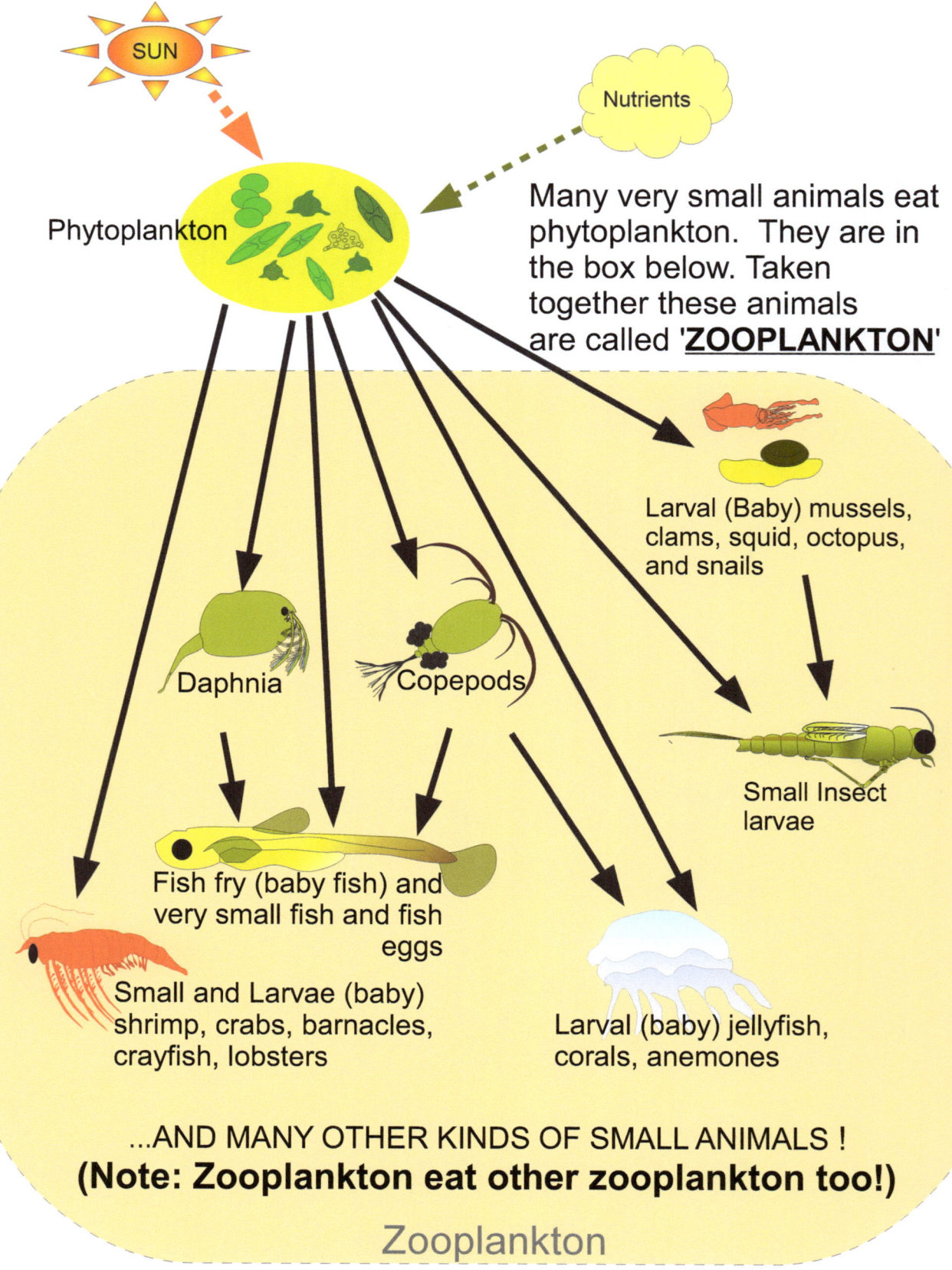

SUN

Nutrients

Phytoplankton

Many very small animals eat phytoplankton. They are in the box below. Taken together these animals are called '**ZOOPLANKTON**'

Larval (Baby) mussels, clams, squid, octopus, and snails

Daphnia

Copepods

Small Insect larvae

Fish fry (baby fish) and very small fish and fish eggs

Small and Larvae (baby) shrimp, crabs, barnacles, crayfish, lobsters

Larval (baby) jellyfish, corals, anemones

...AND MANY OTHER KINDS OF SMALL ANIMALS !
(Note: Zooplankton eat other zooplankton too!)

Zooplankton

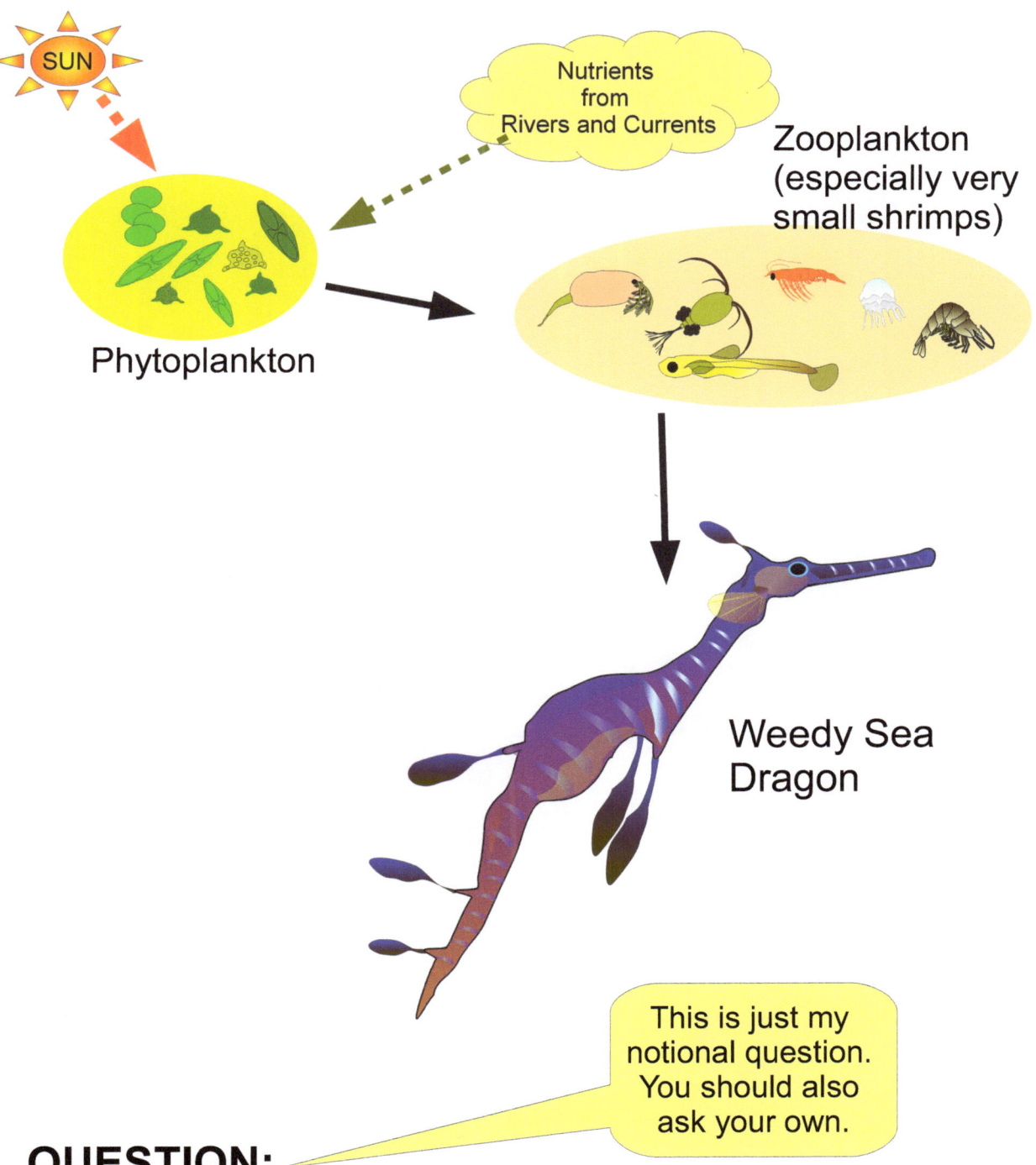

QUESTION:
Weedy Sea Dragons hide in sea grass and sea weeds and have very small mouths they use to vacuum in shrimp. Why do you think they live near areas with rivers that empty into the sea?

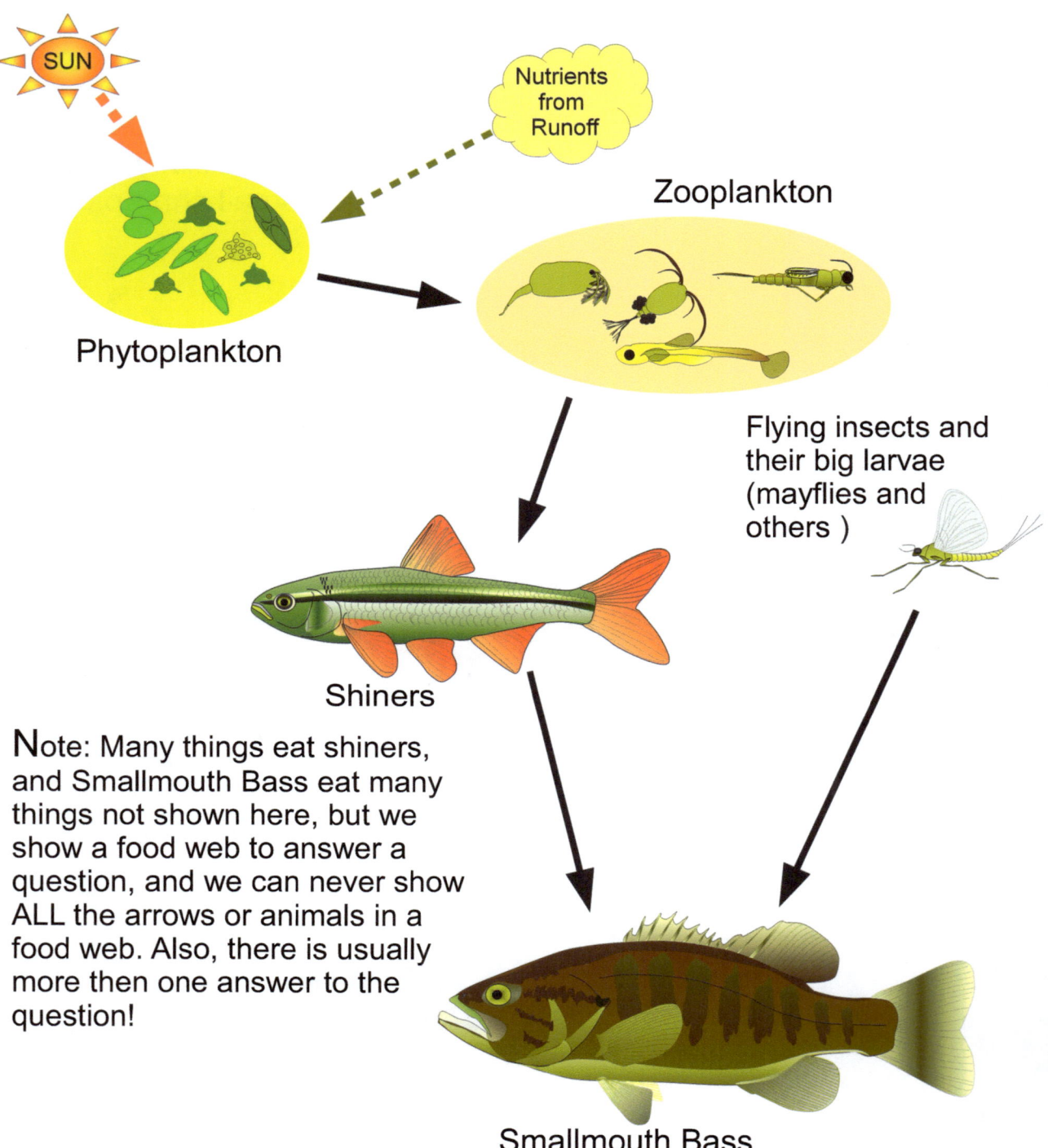

SUN

Nutrients from Runoff

Phytoplankton

Zooplankton

Flying insects and their big larvae (mayflies and others)

Shiners

Note: Many things eat shiners, and Smallmouth Bass eat many things not shown here, but we show a food web to answer a question, and we can never show ALL the arrows or animals in a food web. Also, there is usually more then one answer to the question!

Smallmouth Bass

QUESTION:

If the shiners are hard to catch, what else can smallmouth bass eat?

(Clue: This is why mayfly hatches are good times to fly fish!)

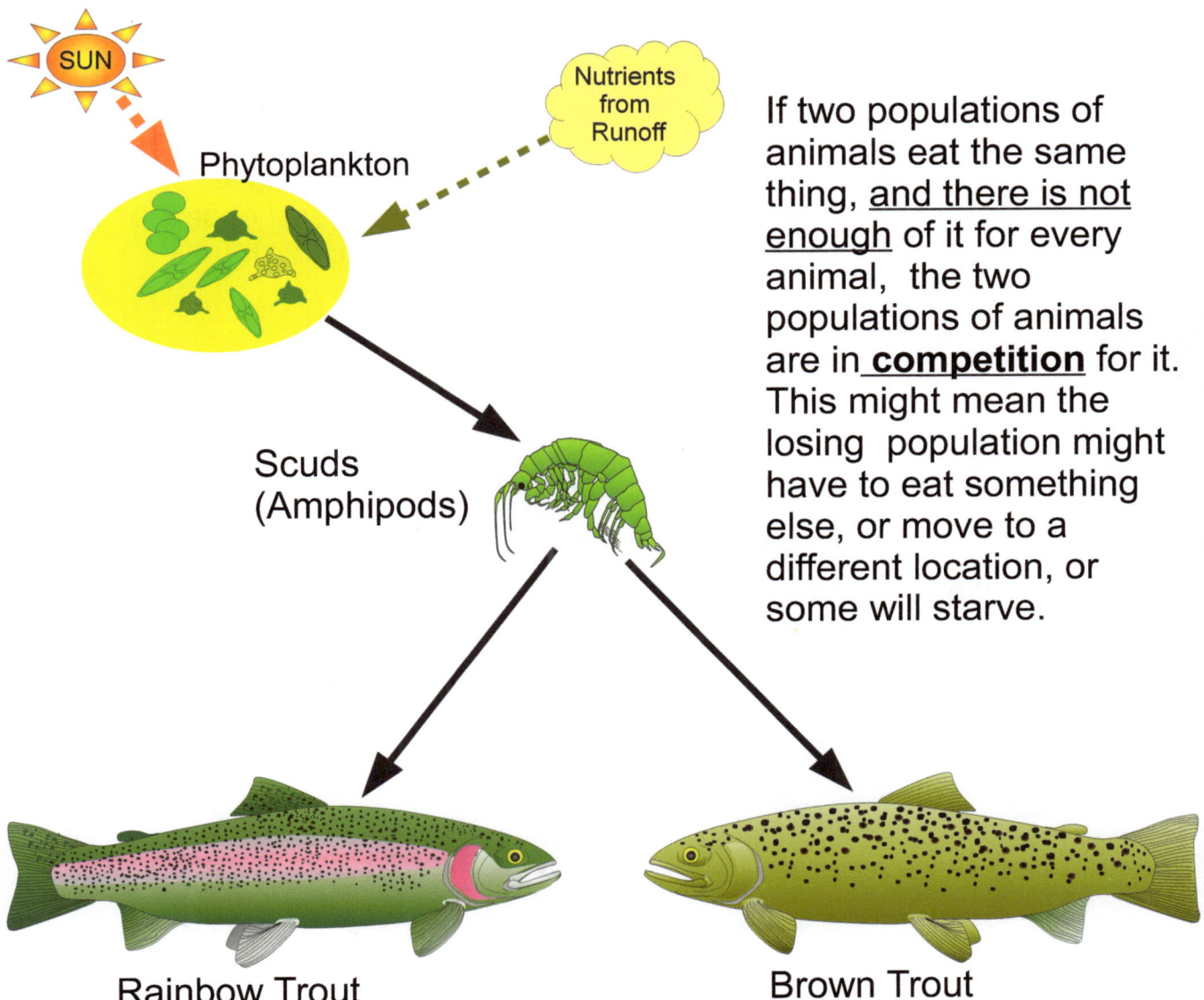

Phytoplankton

Nutrients from Runoff

SUN

Scuds (Amphipods)

If two populations of animals eat the same thing, <u>and there is not enough</u> of it for every animal, the two populations of animals are in **competition** for it. This might mean the losing population might have to eat something else, or move to a different location, or some will starve.

Rainbow Trout

Brown Trout

QUESTIONS:
1) If their are not enough scuds, what two populations (species) are in **competition** here? Over what item (a population of something they both eat, *hint look for two arrows leaving one population*)?

2) If I have a stream where the main fish food is a population of scuds, and I already have a big population of brown trout, what can happen when I add a whole lot of rainbow trout?

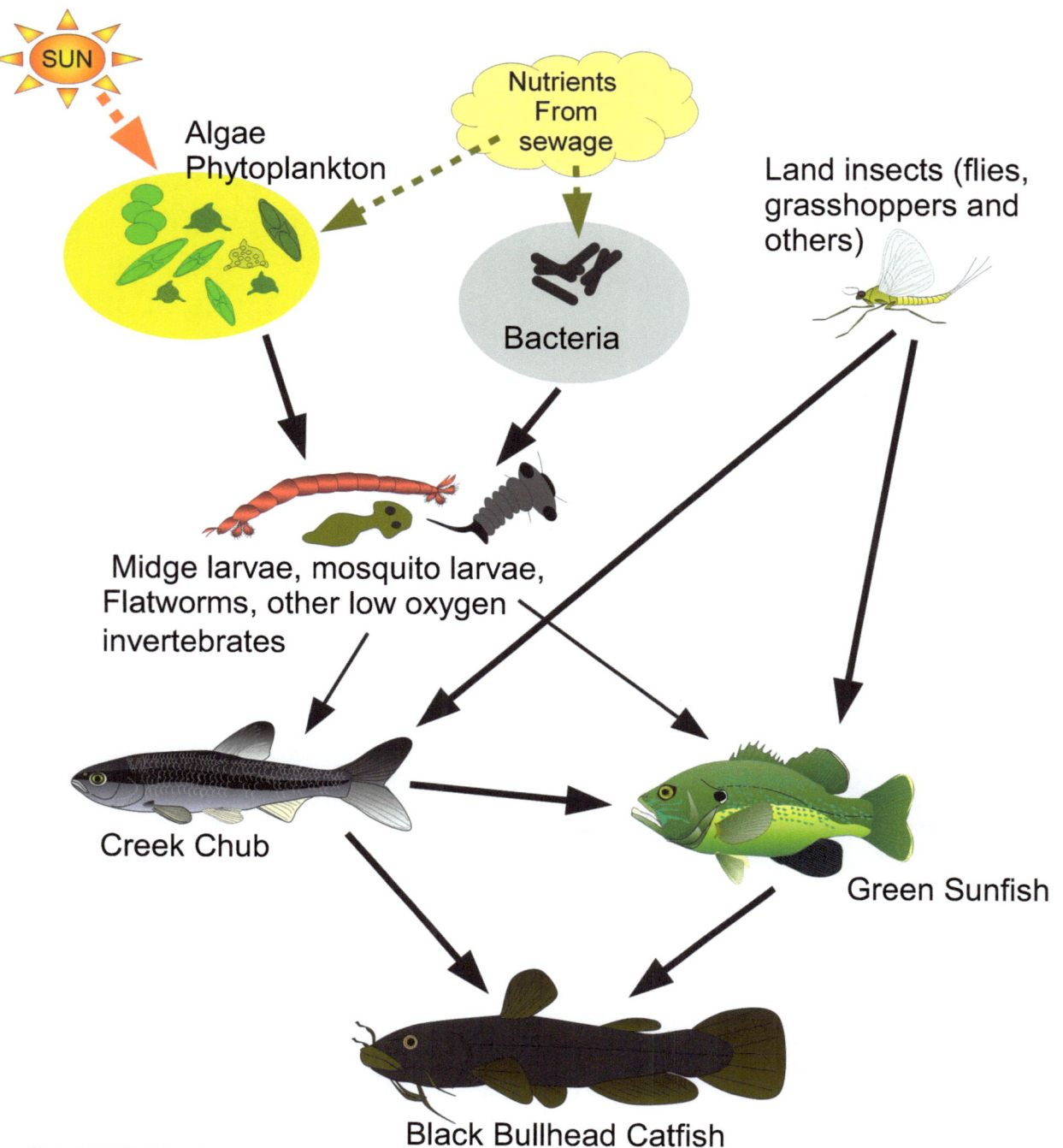

SUN

Algae
Phytoplankton

Nutrients
From
sewage

Bacteria

Land insects (flies,
grasshoppers and
others)

Midge larvae, mosquito larvae,
Flatworms, other low oxygen
invertebrates

Creek Chub

Green Sunfish

Black Bullhead Catfish

QUESTION:

This small creek is very polluted with raw sewage, so it is low in oxygen, but it still has a few fish. What would happen to the fish, food-wise, if all the grass and trees (where land insects live) around the creek are replaced with concrete?

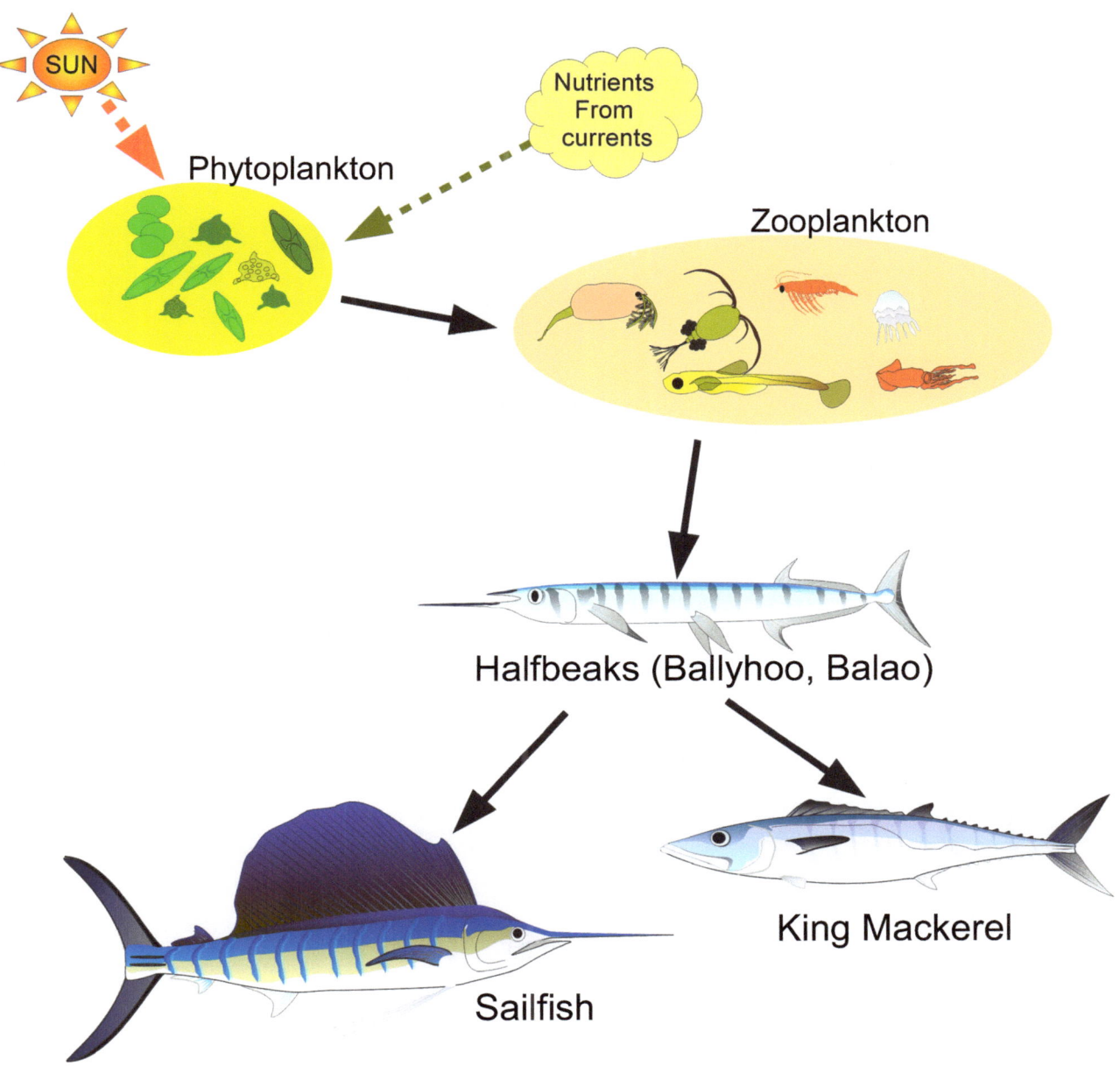

SUN

Nutrients From currents

Phytoplankton

Zooplankton

Halfbeaks (Ballyhoo, Balao)

Sailfish

King Mackerel

QUESTION:

Atlantic Sailfish slash ballyhoo on the surface on the reef edge, and some wounded ballyhoo drop deep below the sails. Why do you think king mackerel sit a little deeper at the reef edge in the same spots as the sailfish?

(Clue: Kings will eat wounded fish.)

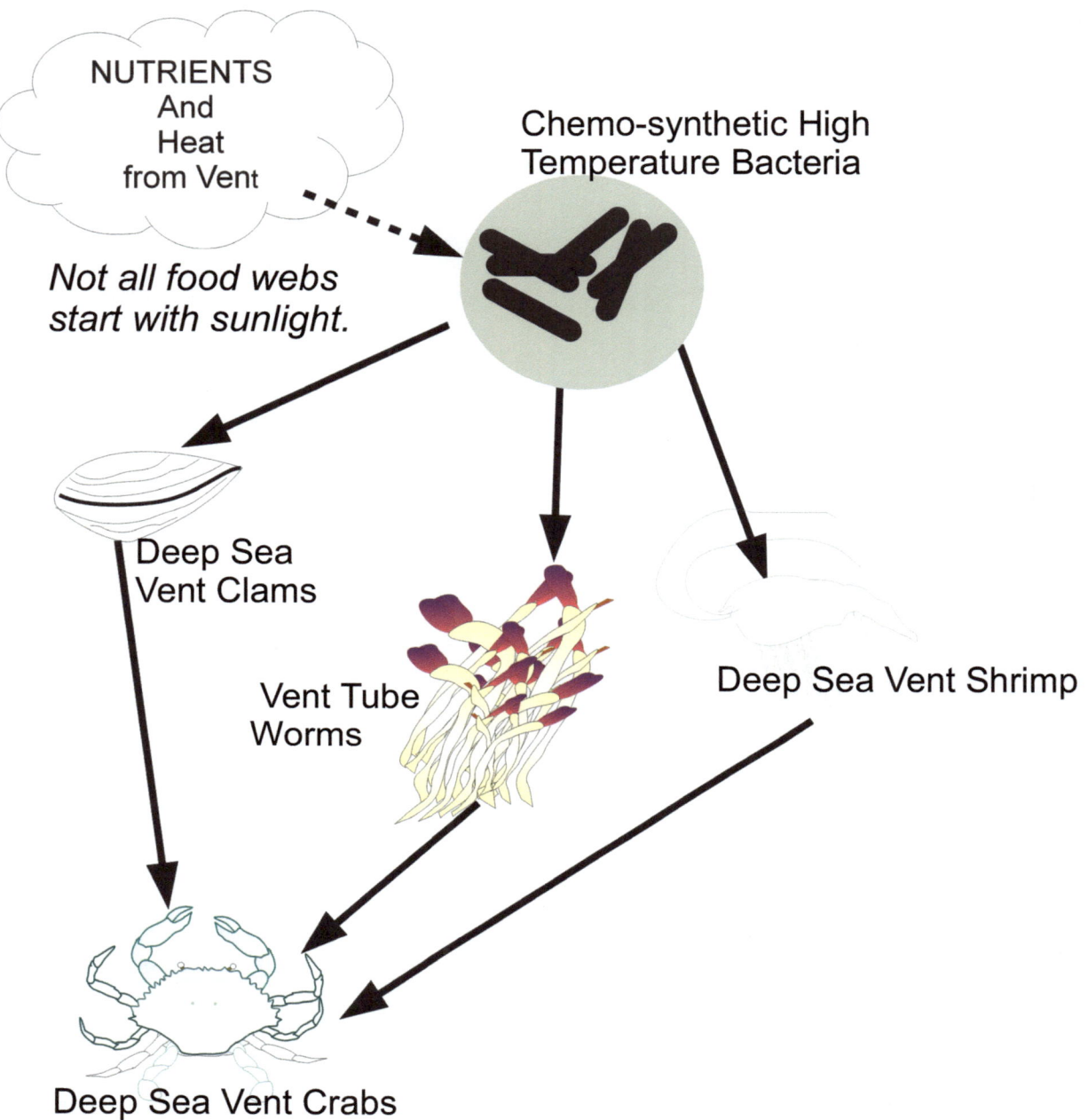

NUTRIENTS
And
Heat
from Vent

*Not all food webs
start with sunlight.*

Chemo-synthetic High
Temperature Bacteria

Deep Sea
Vent Clams

Vent Tube
Worms

Deep Sea Vent Shrimp

Deep Sea Vent Crabs

QUESTION:

Deep Sea Vents are often caused by a 'hot spot' where the Earth's crust is heated and splits to let seawater get hot and enriched with nutrients, then shoot upward. What happens to the crabs if the hot spot moves far away?

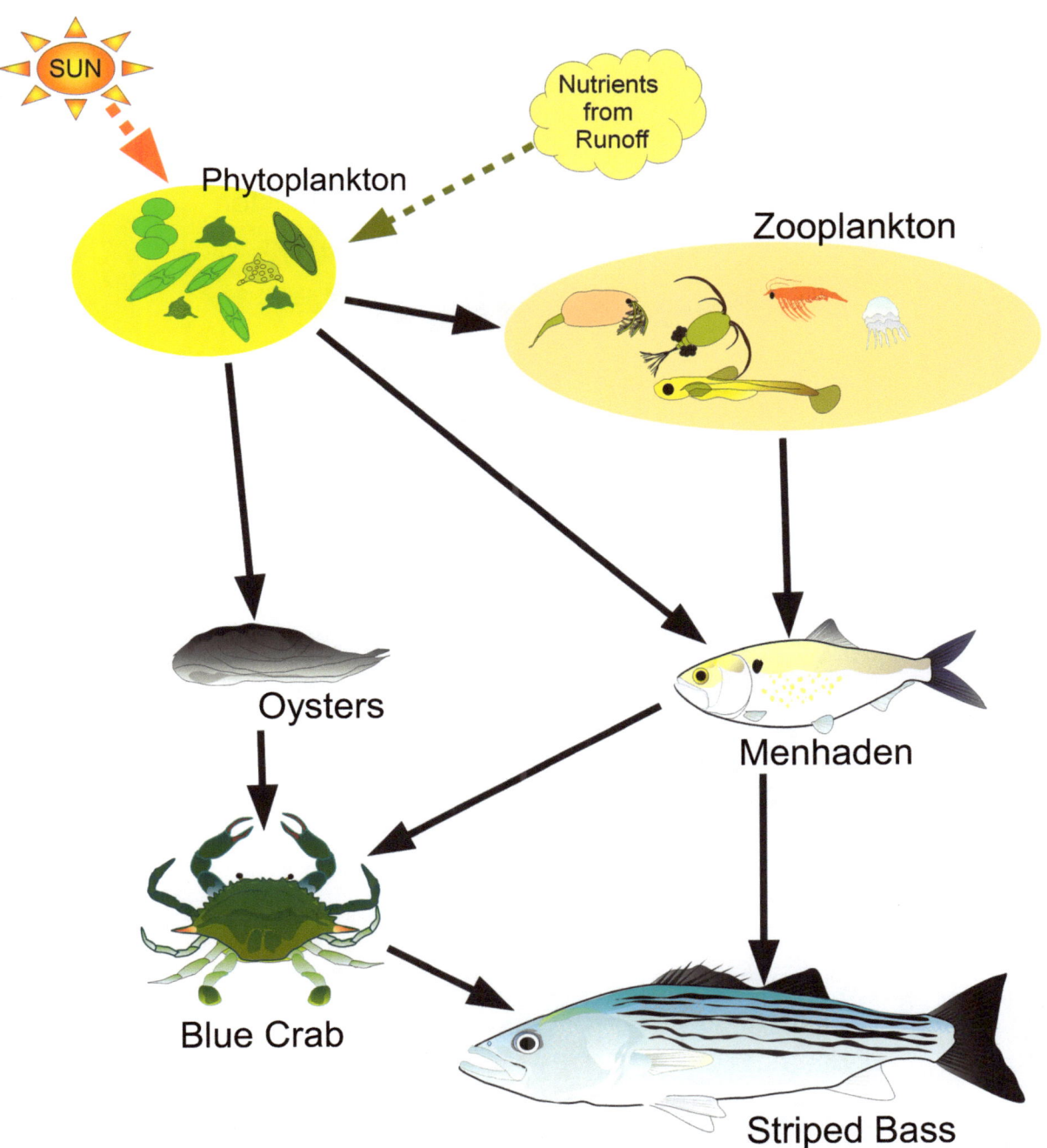

Sun

Nutrients from Runoff

Phytoplankton

Zooplankton

Oysters

Menhaden

Blue Crab

Striped Bass

QUESTION:
Oysters and Blue Crabs are important human food in Chesapeake Bay. Striped Bass are very economically important as game fish. There is often too much phytoplankton in the bay (due to nutrients in runoff), resulting in low oxygen dead zones on the bottom when the algae die, killing oysters. What other role do you think Menhaden serve in keeping crab and bass populations strong, in addition to being food for crabs and bass?

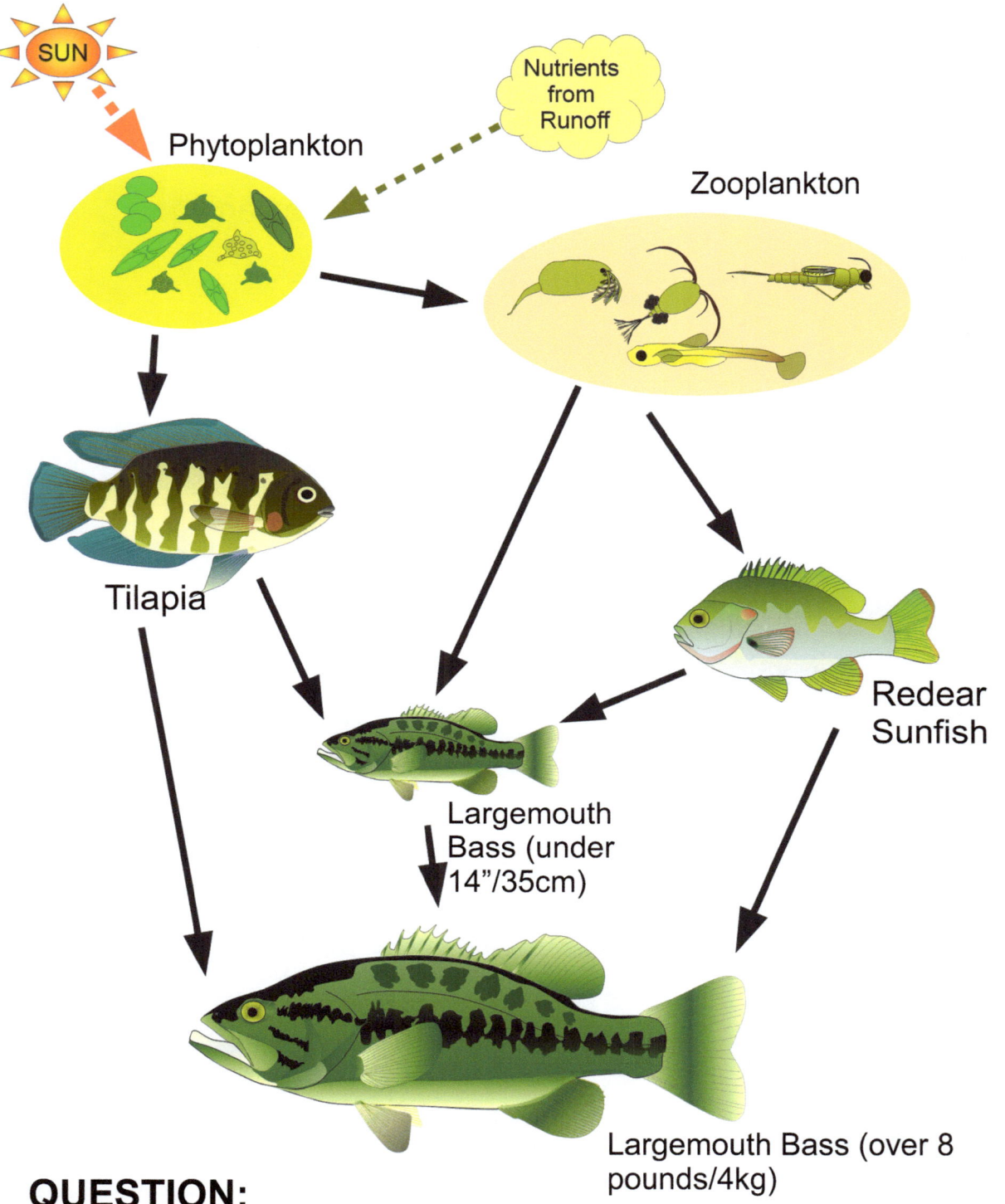

SUN

Phytoplankton

Nutrients from Runoff

Zooplankton

Tilapia

Redear Sunfish

Largemouth Bass (under 14"/35cm)

Largemouth Bass (over 8 pounds/4kg)

QUESTION:
A predator when large can be prey when small. In some ponds in central Florida, there is one or two bass over ten pounds, and there are many remaining bass under 14" and stunted. Why might it be good for overall fishing to keep bass under 14"?

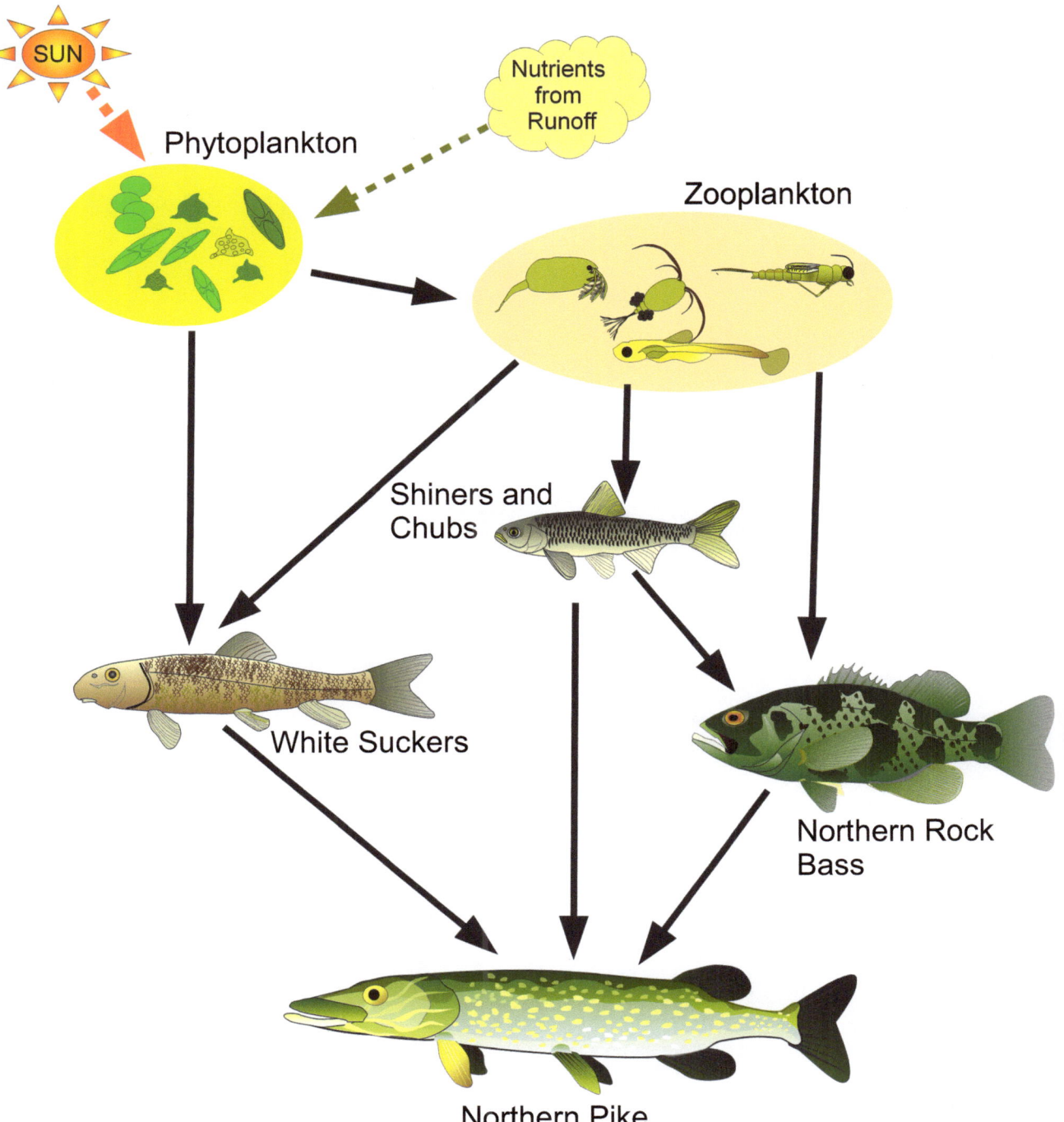

SUN

Nutrients from Runoff

Phytoplankton

Zooplankton

Shiners and Chubs

White Suckers

Northern Rock Bass

Northern Pike

QUESTION:

This creek in northern Indiana feeds Lake Michigan. In the spring, white suckers come up from the lake to spawn, and resident pike prefer to eat suckers over rock bass and minnows. However, why do you think the suckers are a mixed blessing for the rock bass?

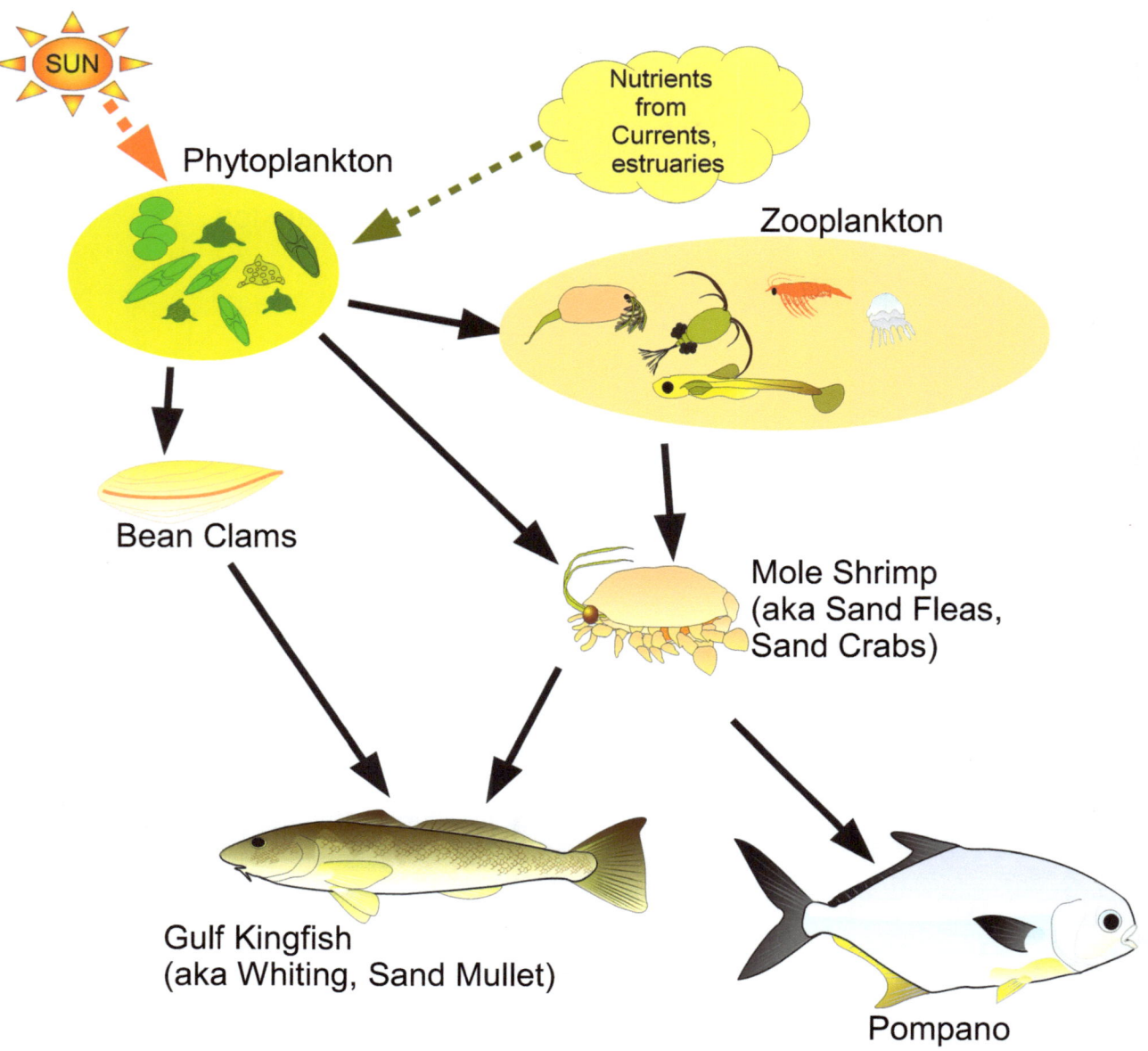

QUESTION:
In the beach surf on the Gulf of Mexico and Atlantic, if I want to catch Pompano, what other fish should I look for, and why?

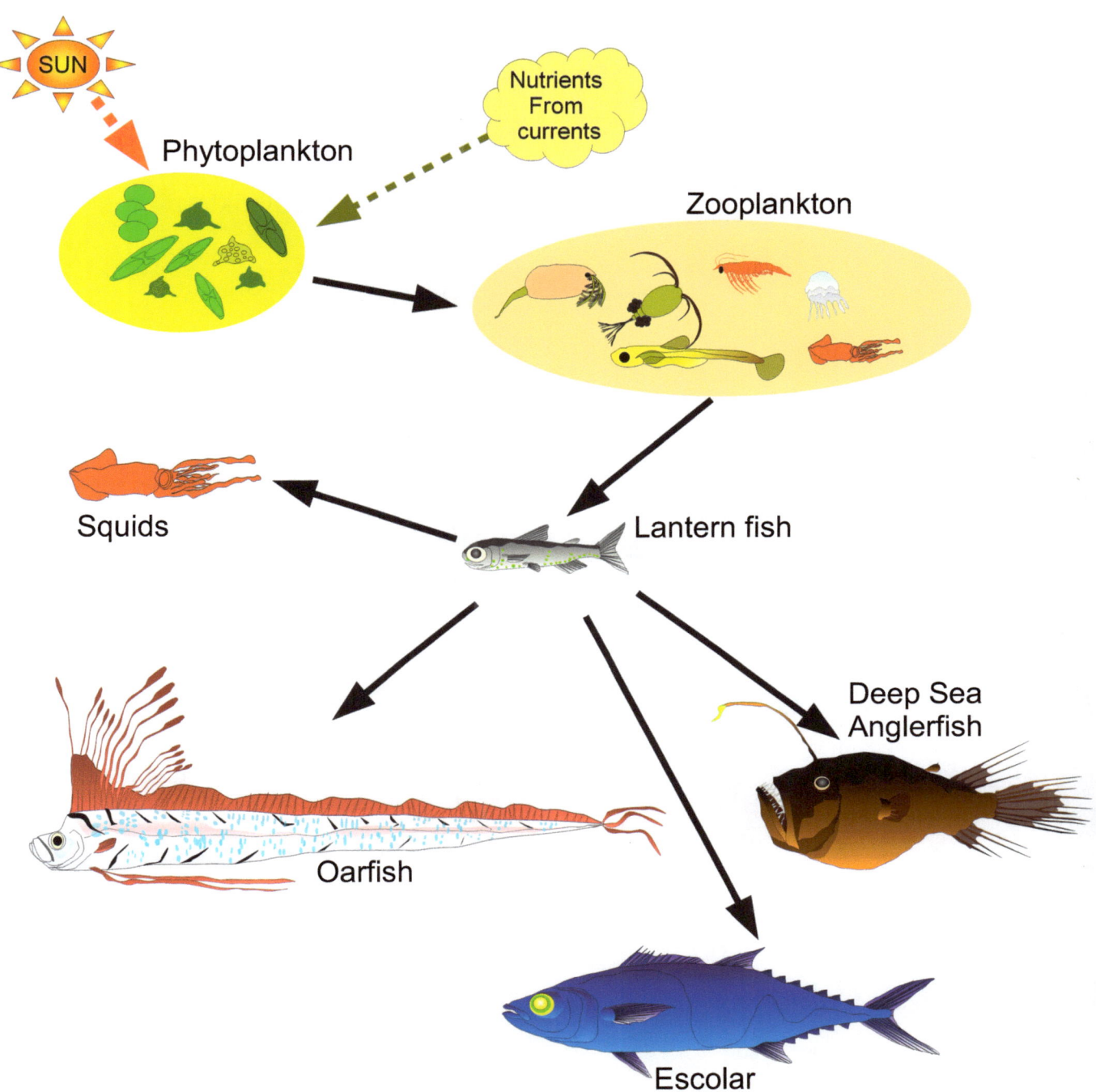

Phytoplankton

SUN

Nutrients From currents

Zooplankton

Squids

Lantern fish

Oarfish

Deep Sea Anglerfish

Escolar

QUESTION:
Why do you think lantern fish are an important deep sea species based on this web?

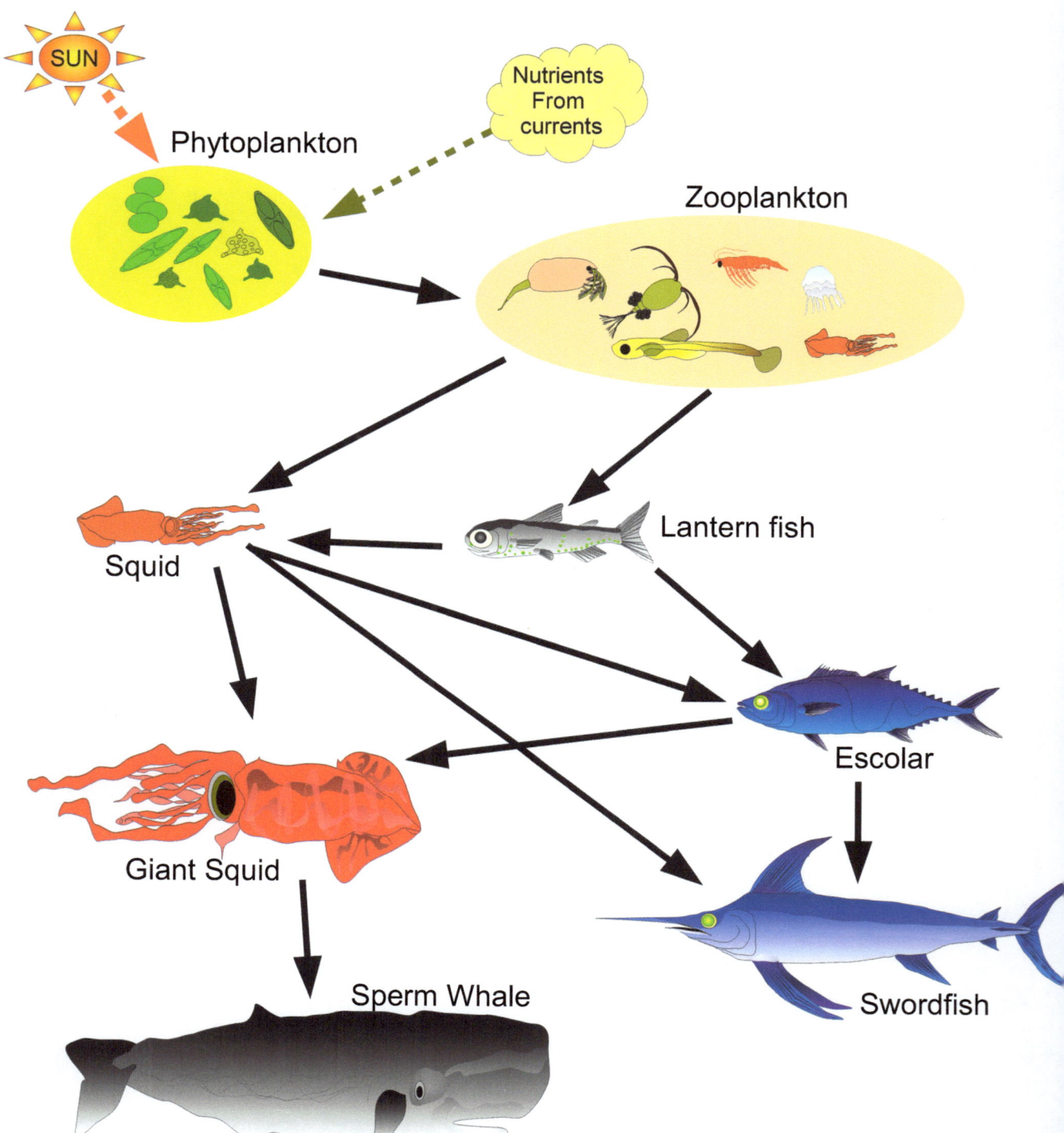

Phytoplankton

SUN

Nutrients From currents

Zooplankton

Squid

Lantern fish

Giant Squid

Escolar

Swordfish

Sperm Whale

QUESTION:

Off Southern Japan I see Sperm Whales breaching after long dives. Escolar are in the local fish market. What other large animals should I look for deep below my boat?

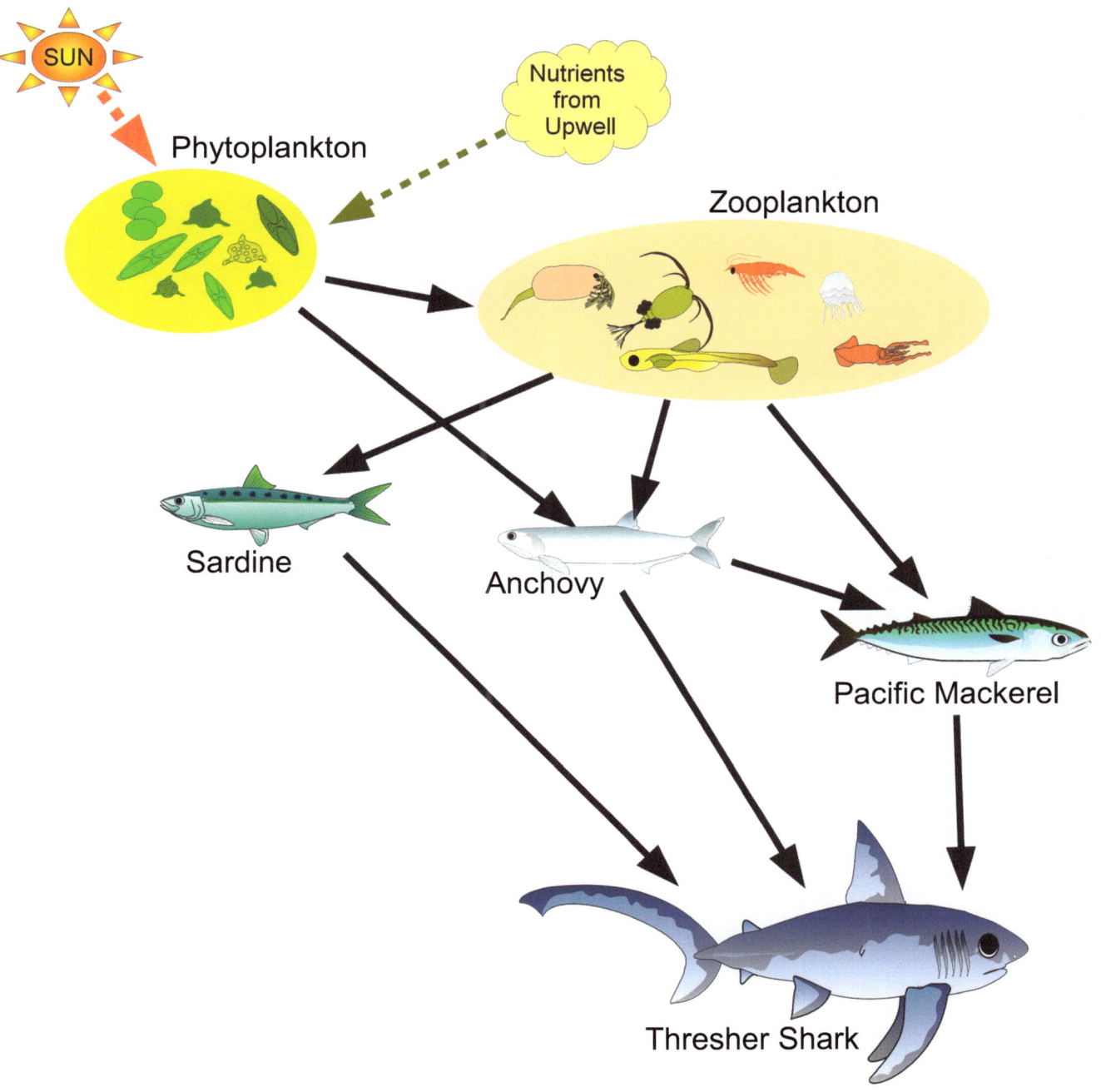

QUESTION:

I see an area of green on the surface of an up-well offshore of southern California in the spring. To find Thresher sharks, what small fish should be schooling and feeding near the green area?

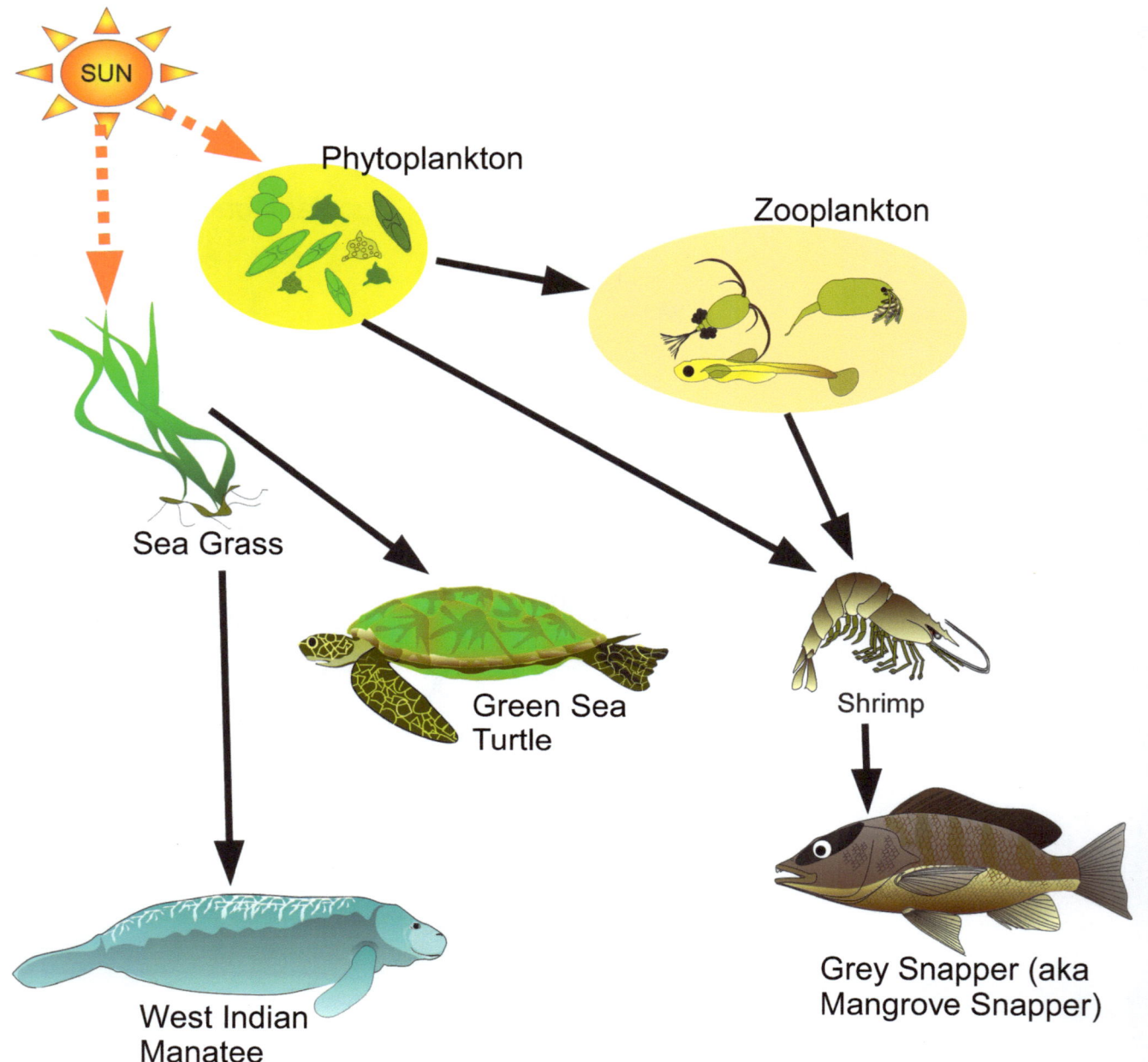

Sun

Phytoplankton

Zooplankton

Sea Grass

Green Sea Turtle

Shrimp

West Indian Manatee

Grey Snapper (aka Mangrove Snapper)

QUESTION:
Shrimp hide in sea grass. Why do you think Grey Snappers follow Manatees and maybe turtles?

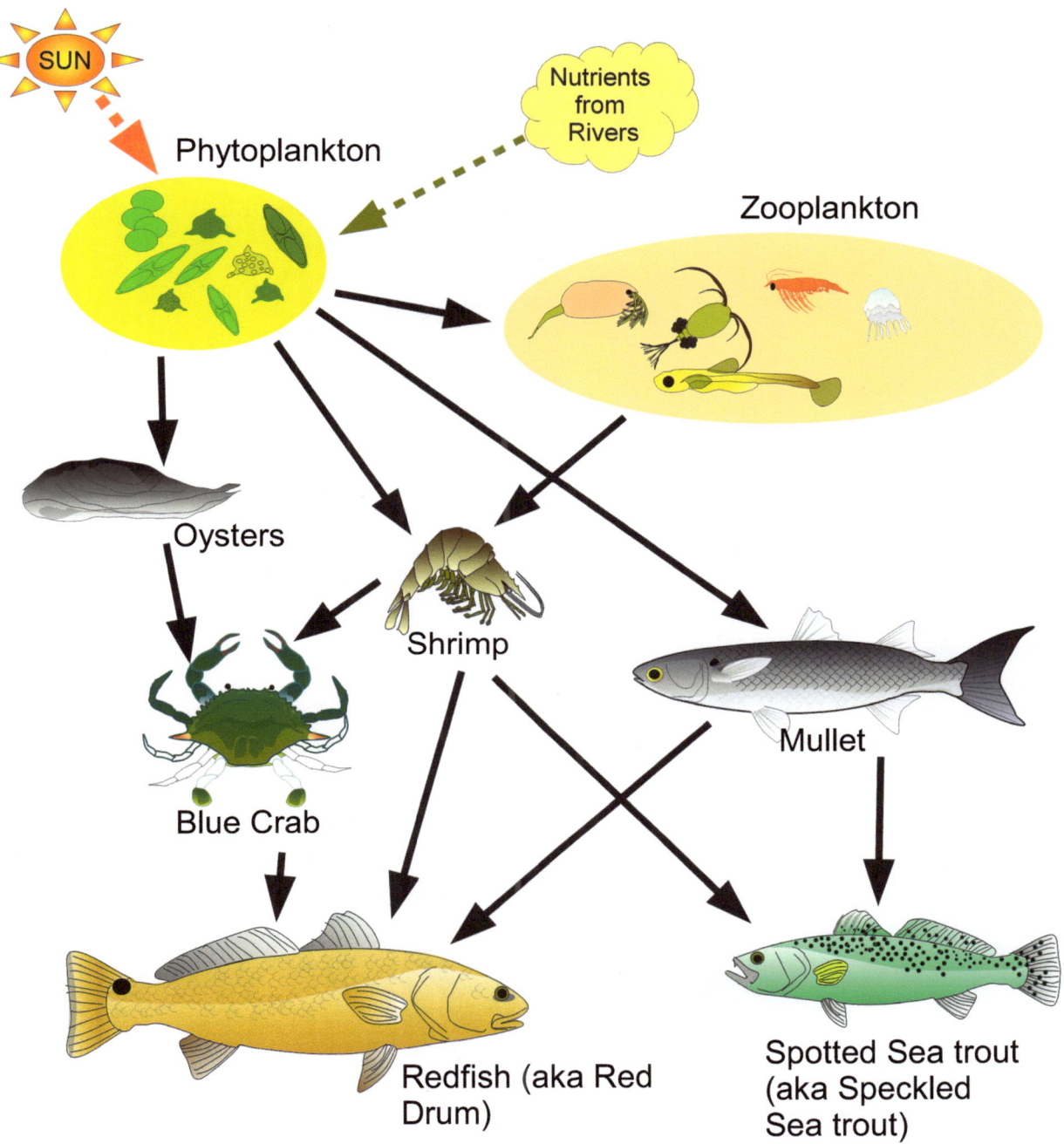

QUESTION:
Assume Redfish and Sea trout like to be near multiple food sources. Should I look for crabs or mullet first to find the Redfish and sea trout?

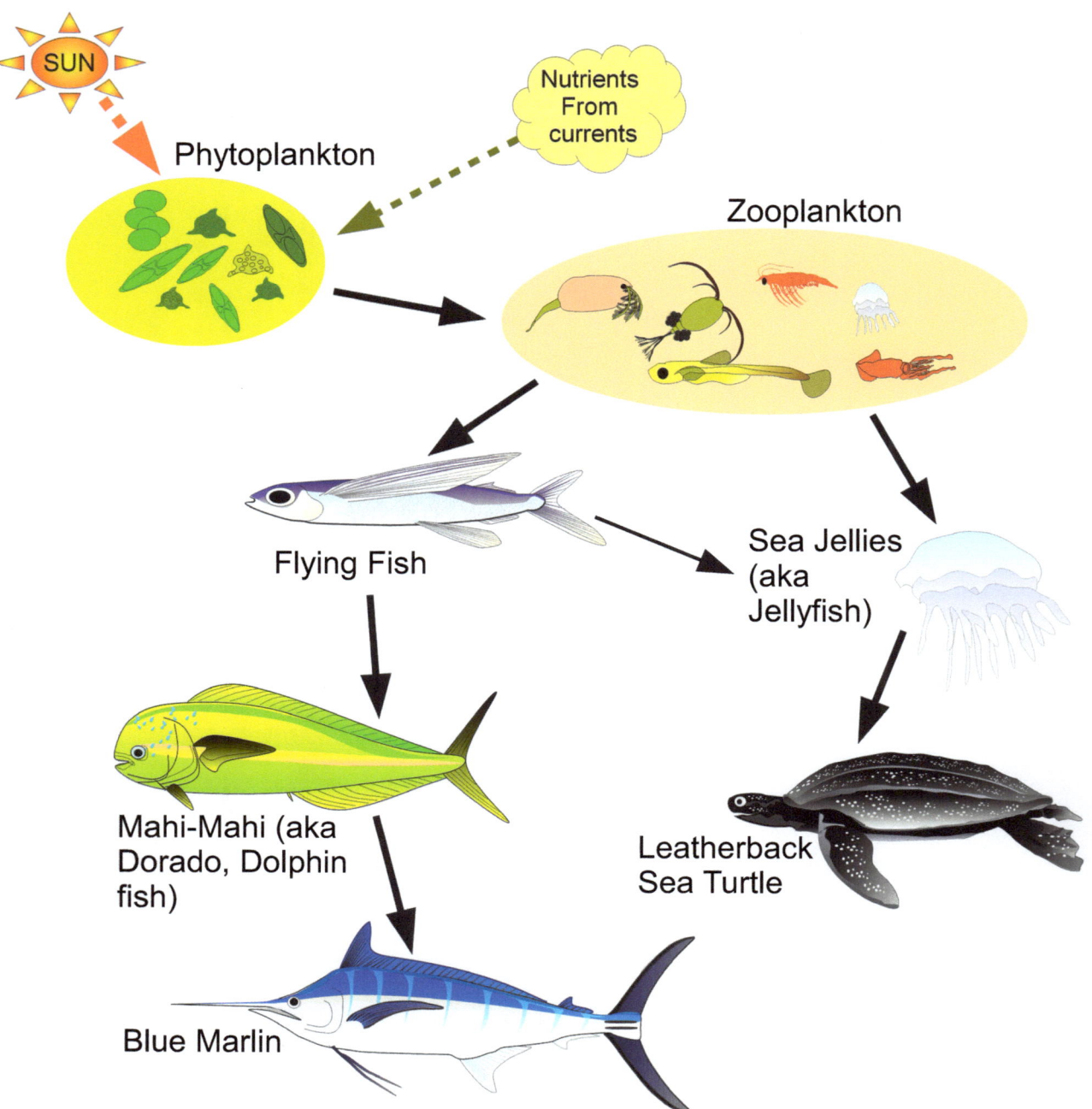

Phytoplankton

SUN

Nutrients From currents

Zooplankton

Flying Fish

Sea Jellies (aka Jellyfish)

Mahi-Mahi (aka Dorado, Dolphin fish)

Leatherback Sea Turtle

Blue Marlin

QUESTION:

If I want good populations of blue marlin long term, why should I also want lots of leatherback sea turtles?

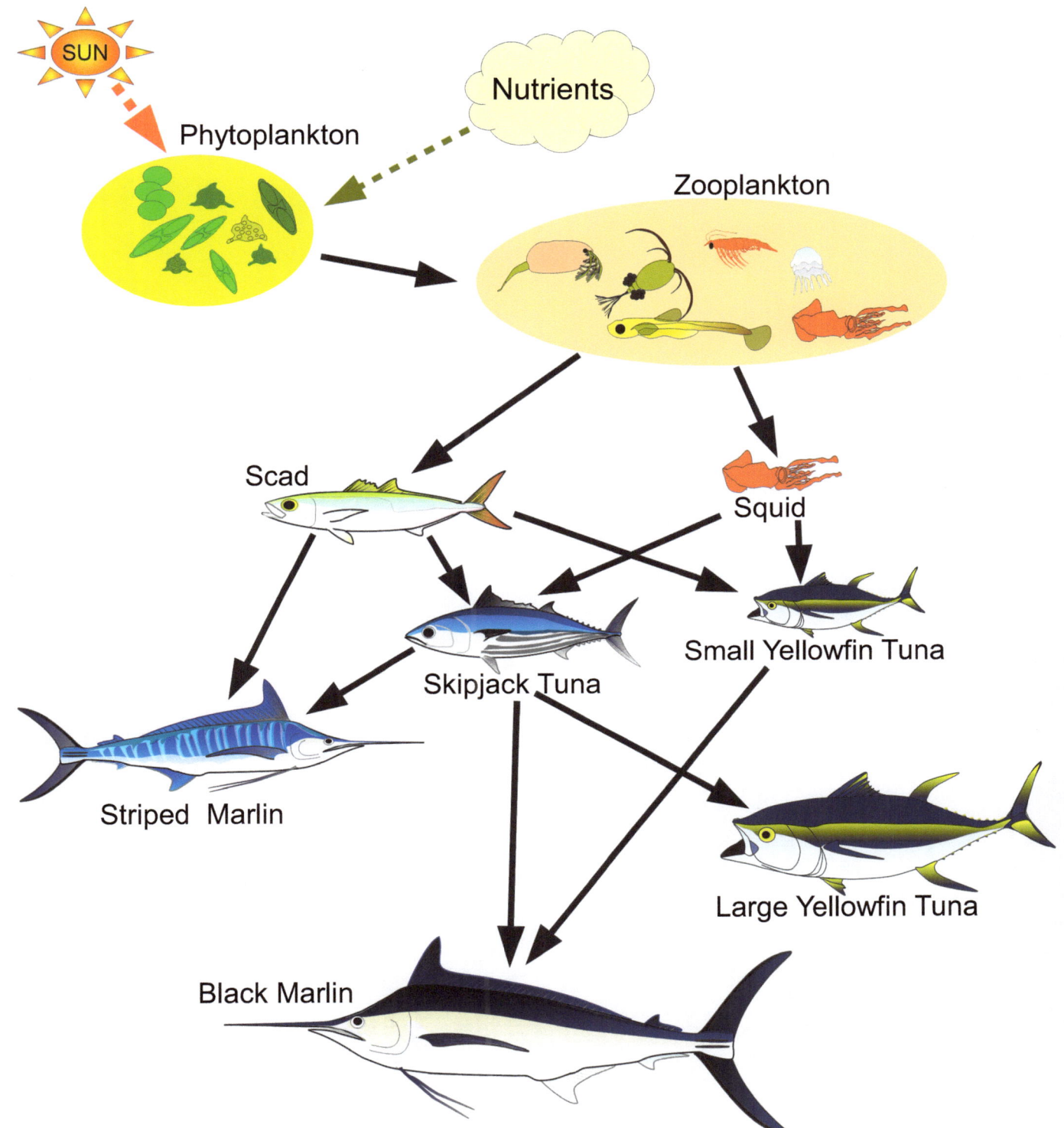

QUESTION:

In the Pacific off of Mexico, seining has removed many skipjack tuna, and while marlin are still present, why over time have my small yellowfin tuna populations dropped off? (Note: Many possible answers.)

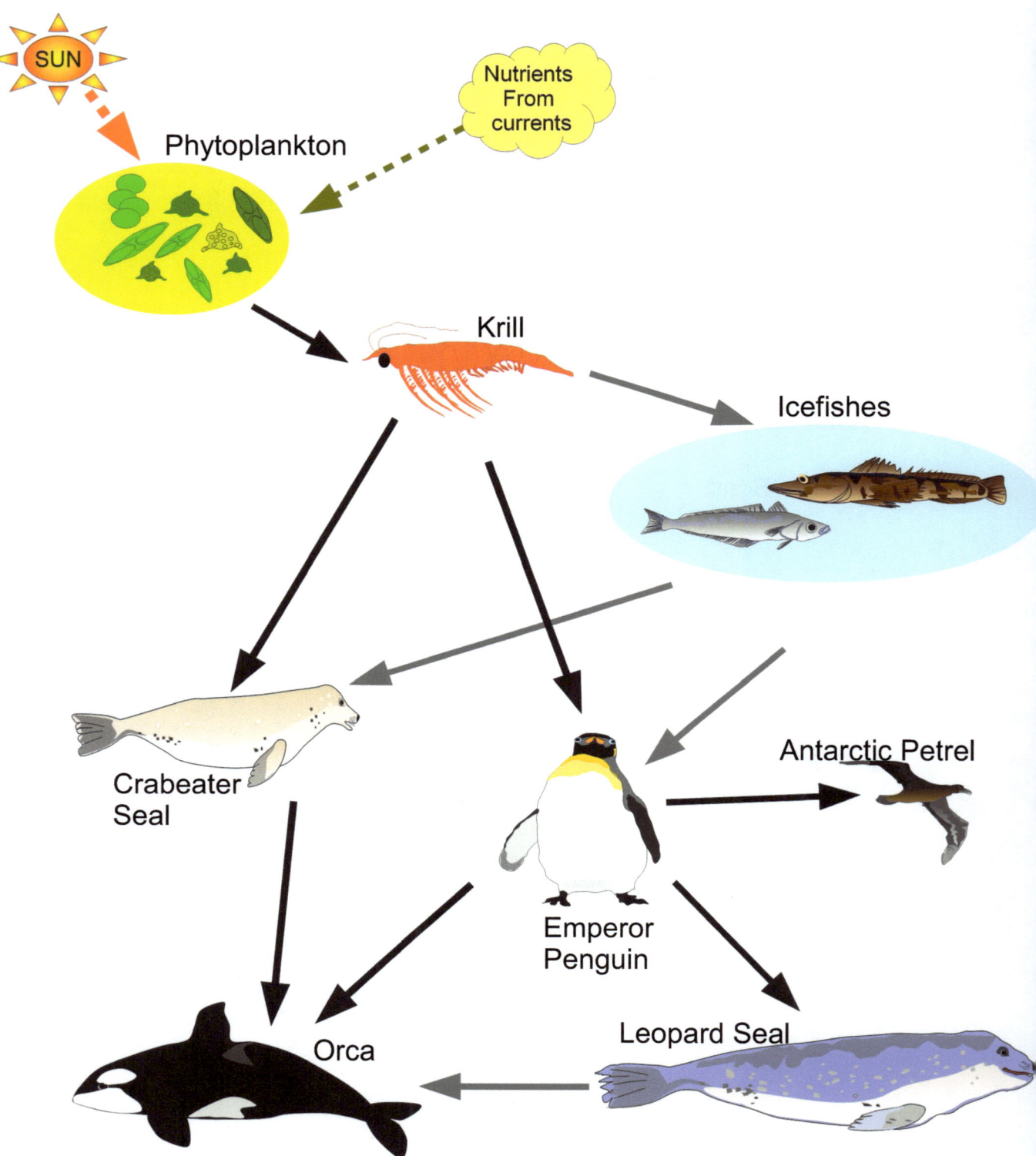

QUESTION:
If krill become rare, what do you think
happens to leopard seal populations?

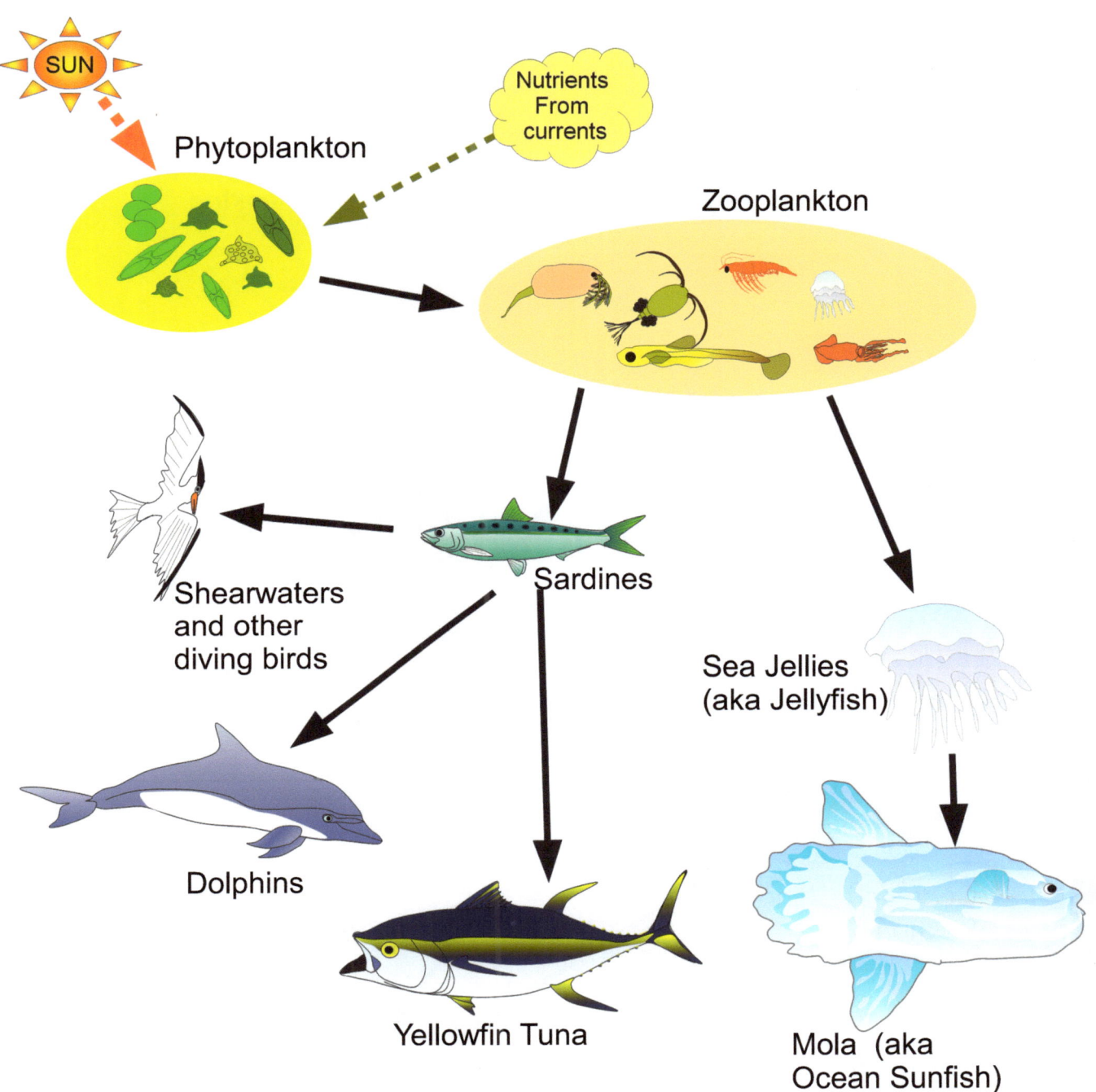

SUN

Phytoplankton

Nutrients From currents

Zooplankton

Shearwaters and other diving birds

Sardines

Sea Jellies (aka Jellyfish)

Dolphins

Yellowfin Tuna

Mola (aka Ocean Sunfish)

QUESTION:

In the up-wells off of sea mounts, a smart tuna boat captain looks for birds, but also for basking molas, and dolphins. Why?

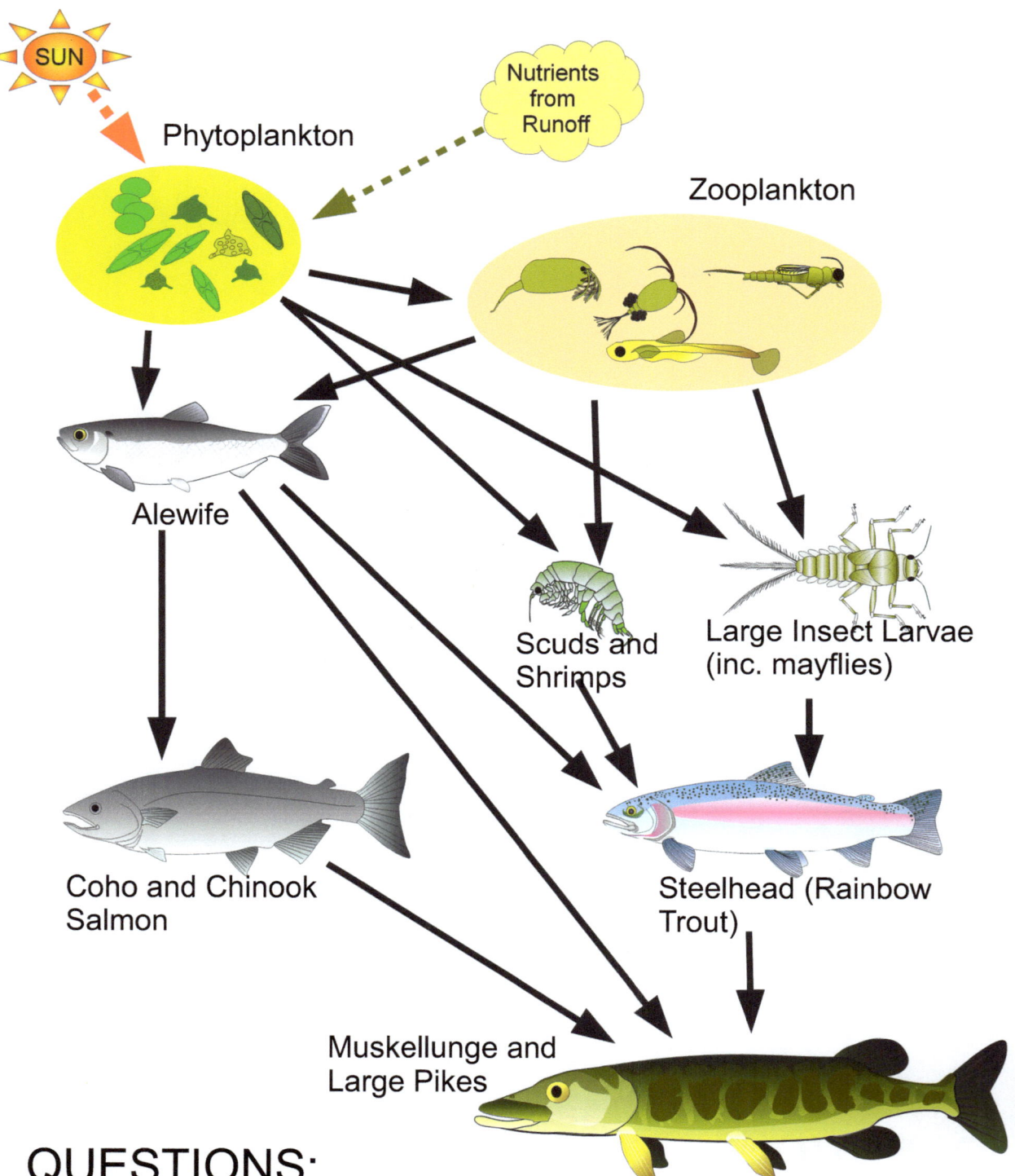

Phytoplankton

SUN

Nutrients from Runoff

Zooplankton

Alewife

Scuds and Shrimps

Large Insect Larvae (inc. mayflies)

Coho and Chinook Salmon

Steelhead (Rainbow Trout)

Muskellunge and Large Pikes

QUESTIONS:
Even though alewife populations drop in some Great Lakes resulting in smaller salmon, steelhead populations seem to be doing well. Why?

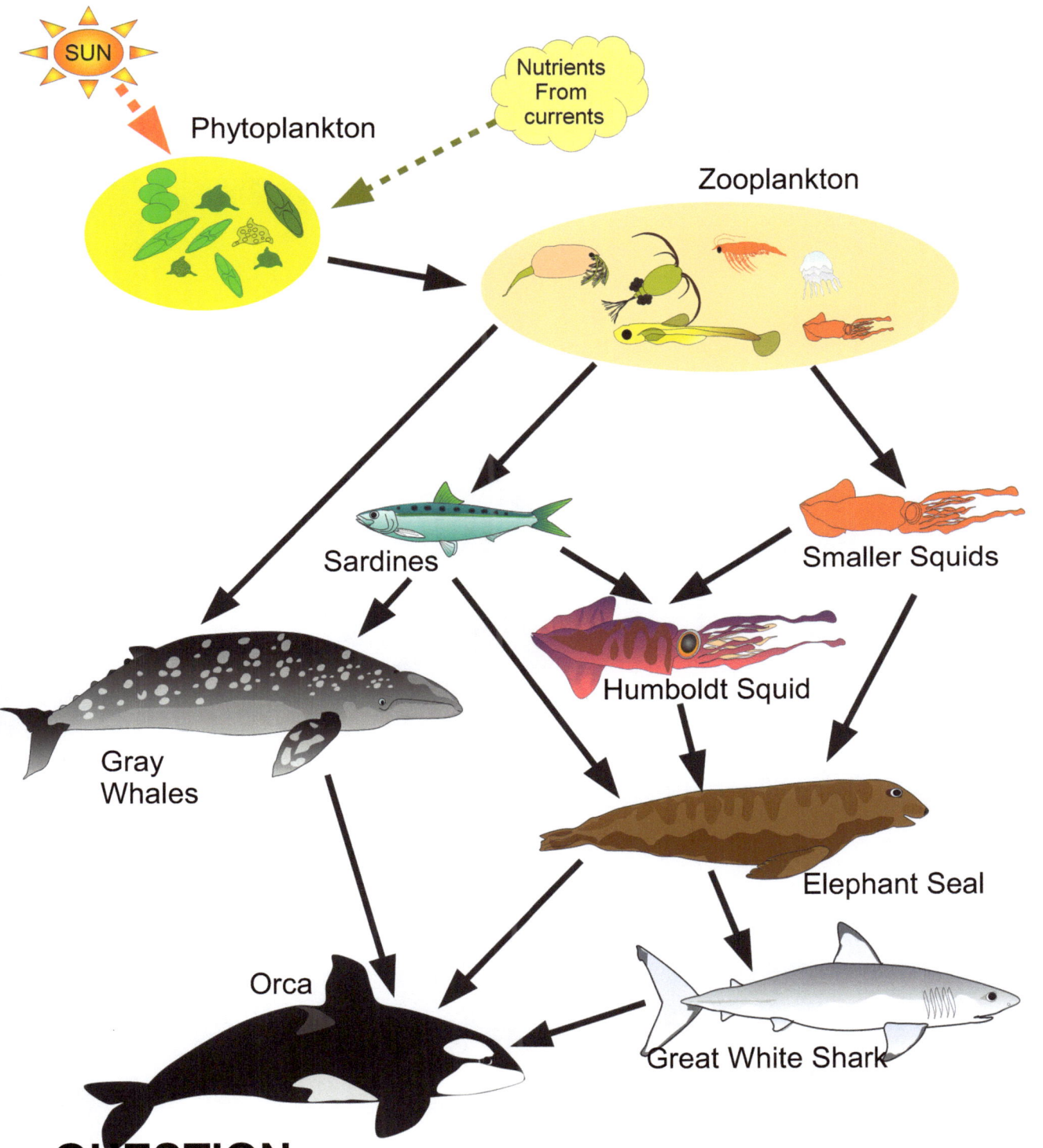

Phytoplankton

SUN

Nutrients From currents

Zooplankton

Sardines

Smaller Squids

Humboldt Squid

Gray Whales

Elephant Seal

Orca

Great White Shark

QUESTION:
Orcas and white sharks in California prefer elephant seals when the seals gather in the spring. Why do you think orcas will kill any great white shark near the seals, even if the orcas don't always eat them?

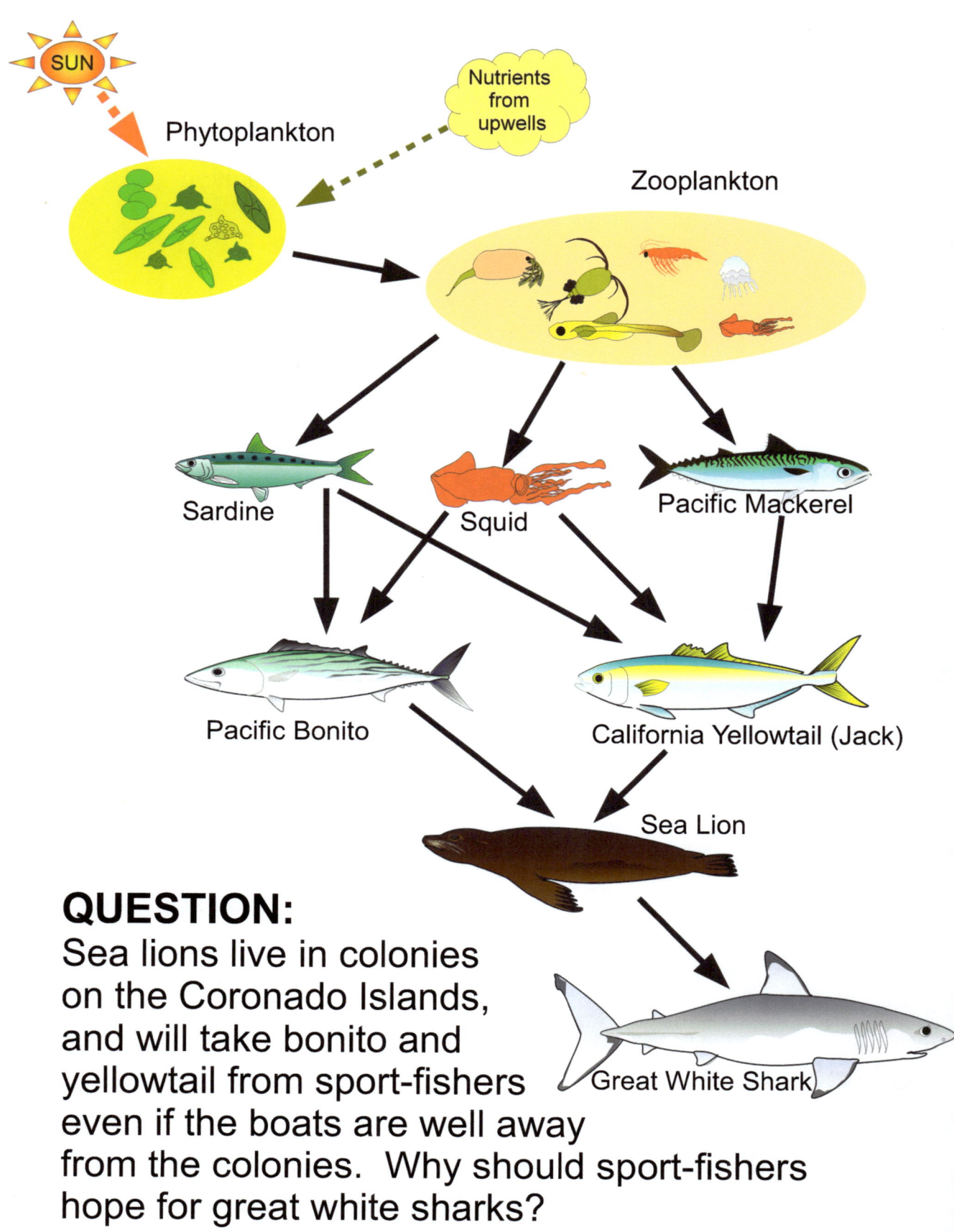

SUN

Phytoplankton

Nutrients from upwells

Zooplankton

Sardine

Squid

Pacific Mackerel

Pacific Bonito

California Yellowtail (Jack)

Sea Lion

Great White Shark

QUESTION:
Sea lions live in colonies on the Coronado Islands, and will take bonito and yellowtail from sport-fishers even if the boats are well away from the colonies. Why should sport-fishers hope for great white sharks?

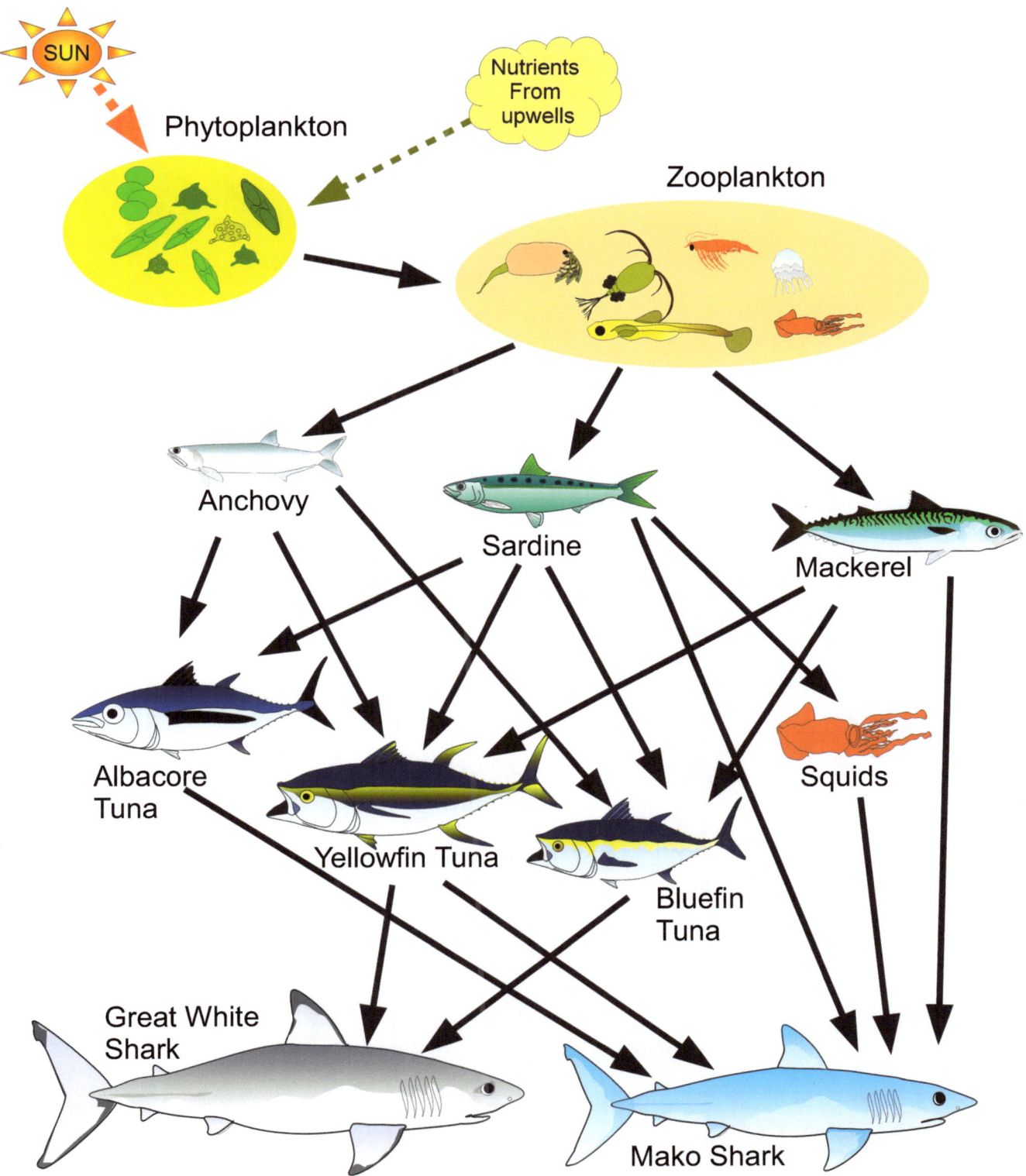

QUESTION:
Tunas are migratory, so not always present in this location. Given this web, which shark would you expect to see even if the tunas are not around?

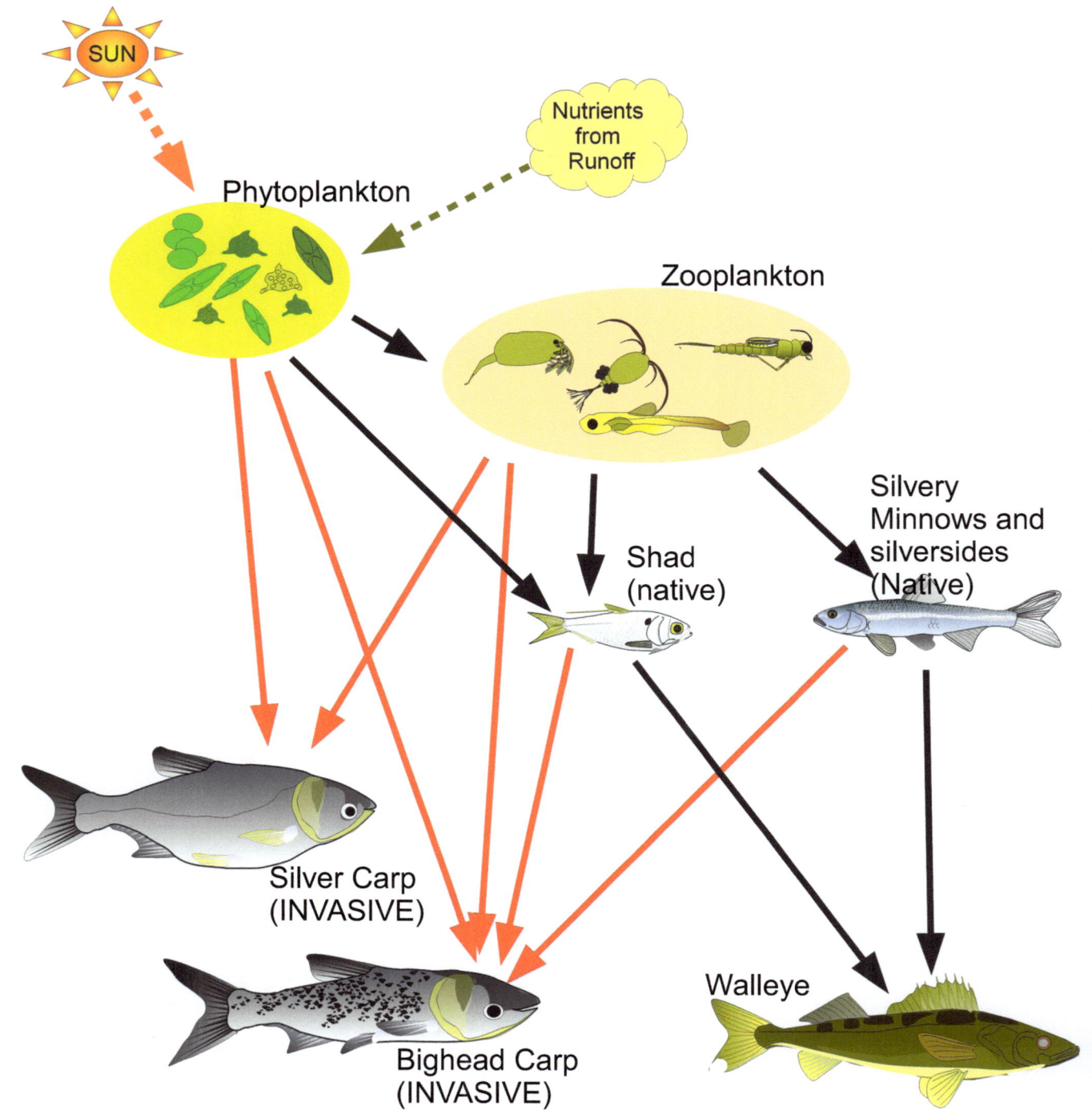

QUESTION:
Why should walleye populations be affected by the silver and bighead carp invasion?

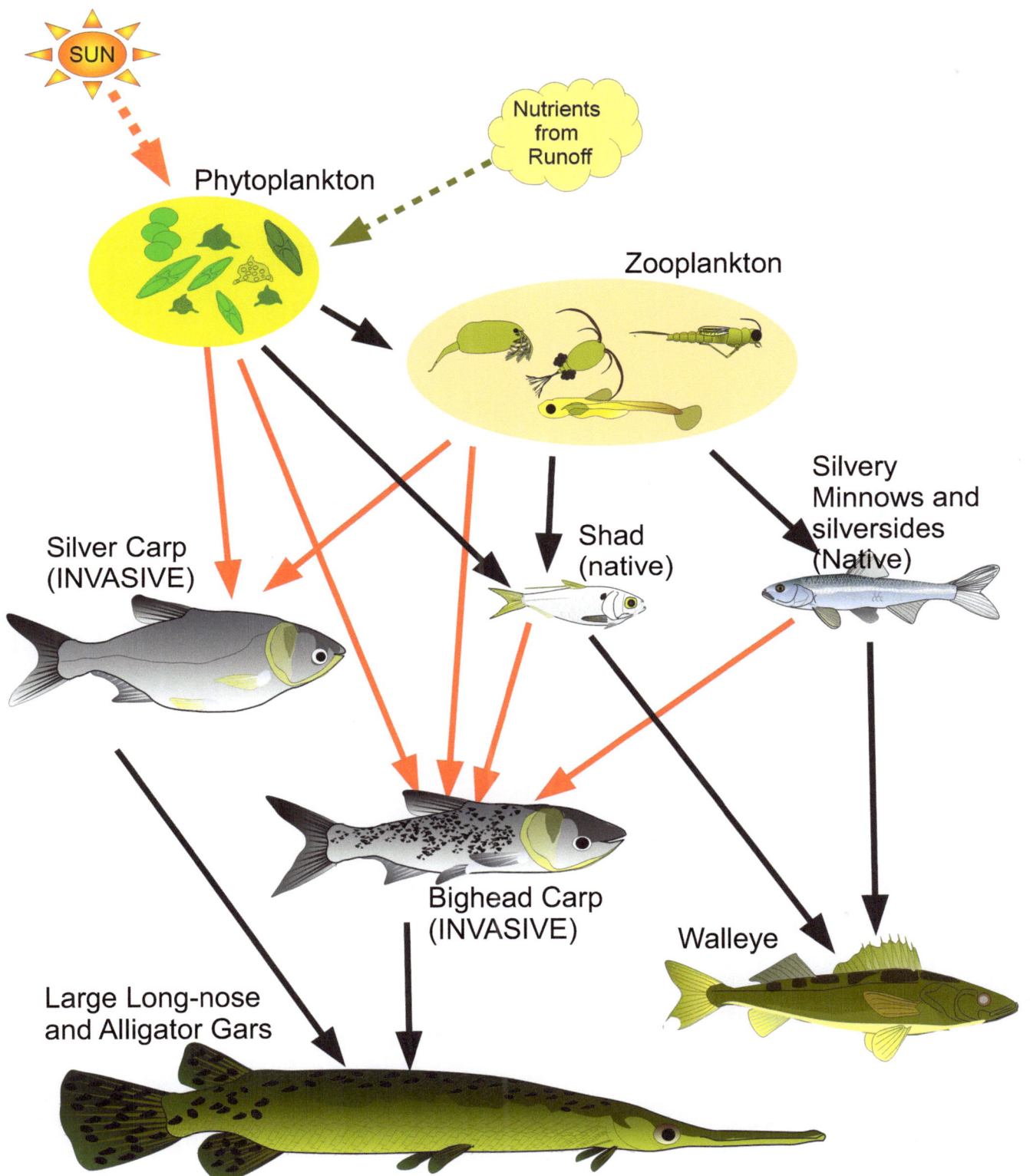

QUESTION:
How would having more large Gars affect Walleye populations here?

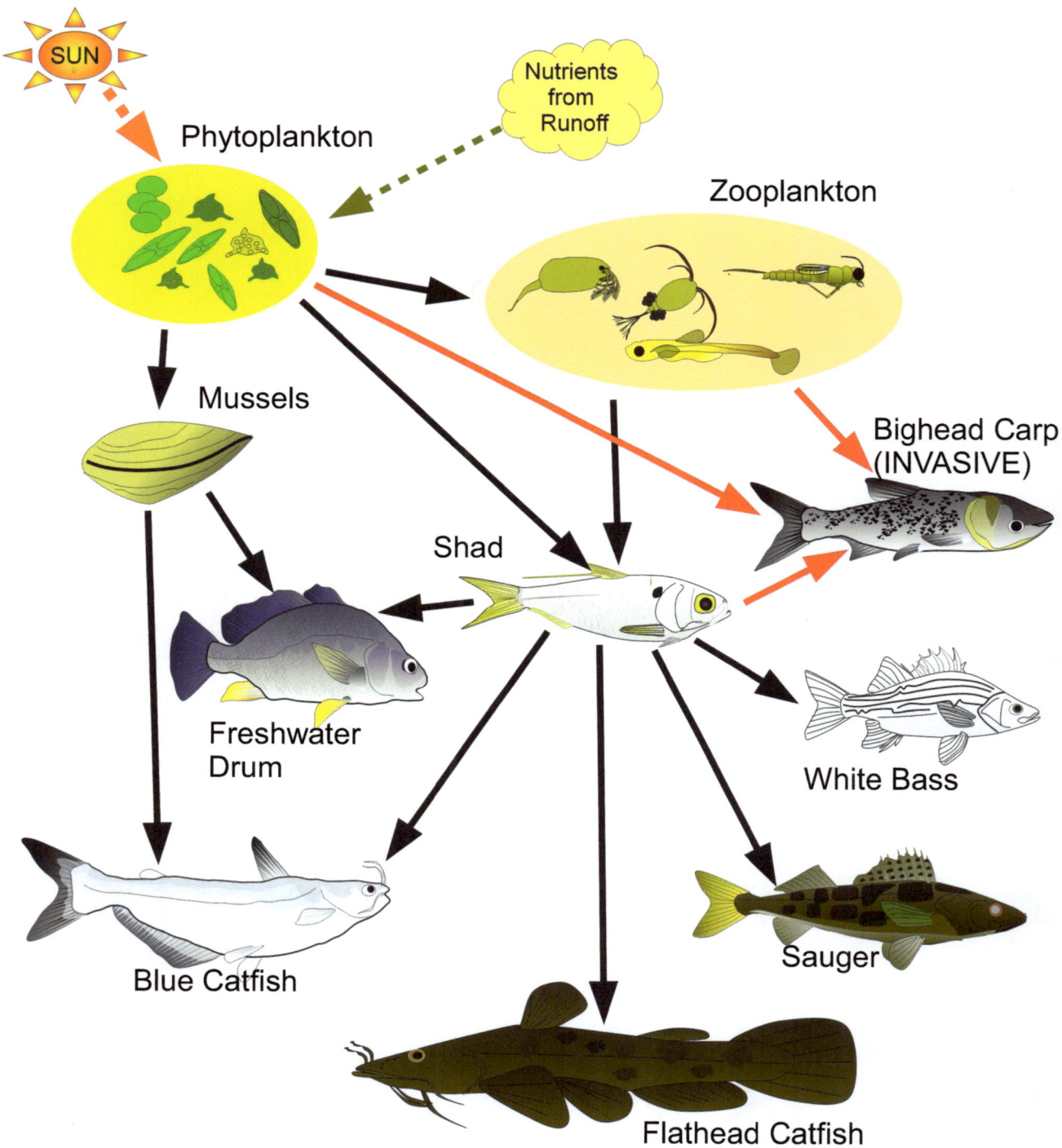

SUN

Nutrients from Runoff

Phytoplankton

Zooplankton

Mussels

Bighead Carp (INVASIVE)

Shad

Freshwater Drum

White Bass

Blue Catfish

Sauger

Flathead Catfish

QUESTION:
Shad in this web are key species, but what are two ways bighead carp affect blue catfish populations?

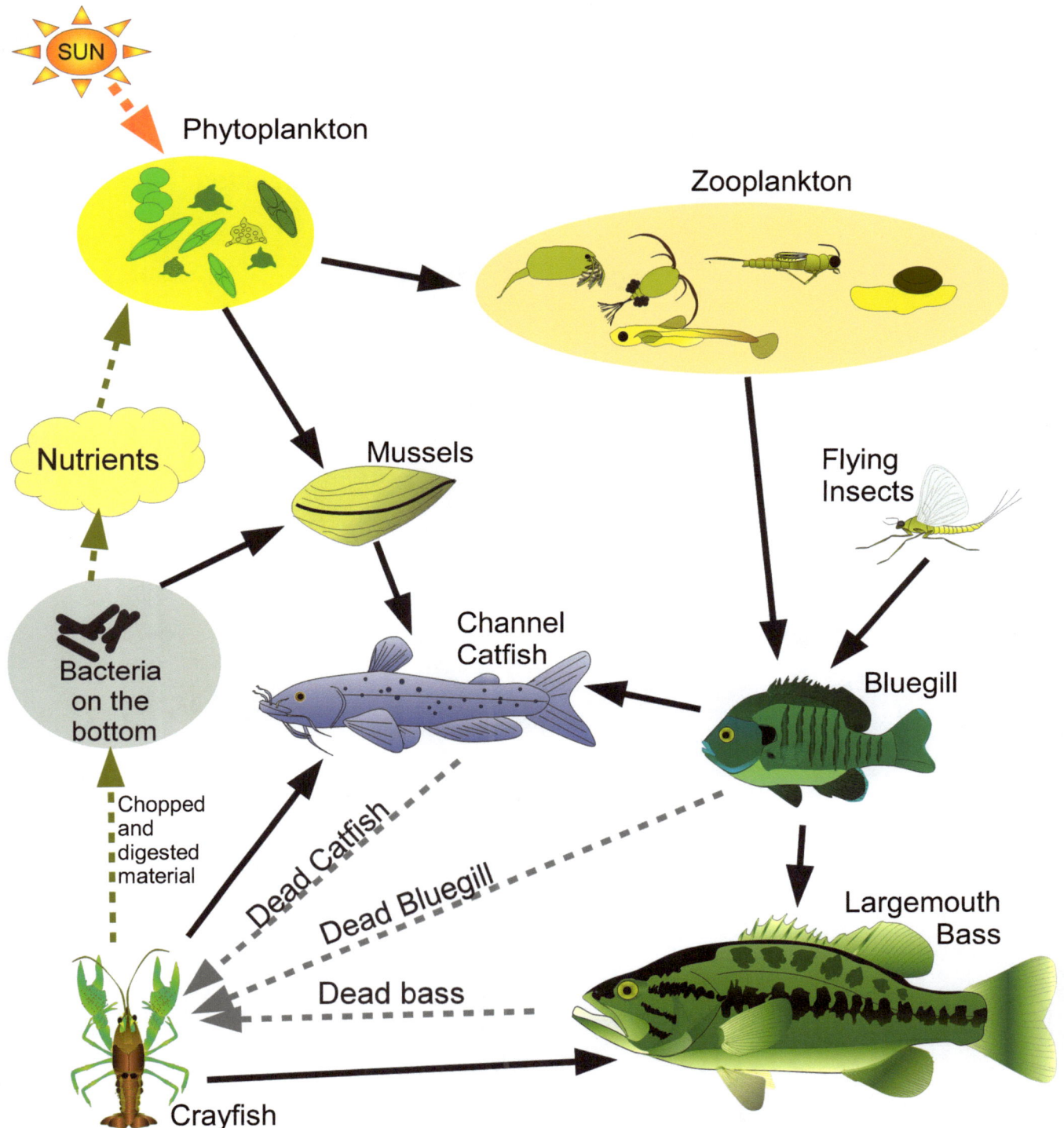

QUESTION:

Crayfish are good at eating dead material and chopping it up for other animals in the process of eating. In this pond, what role do crayfish play in recycling nutrients for mussels and fish?

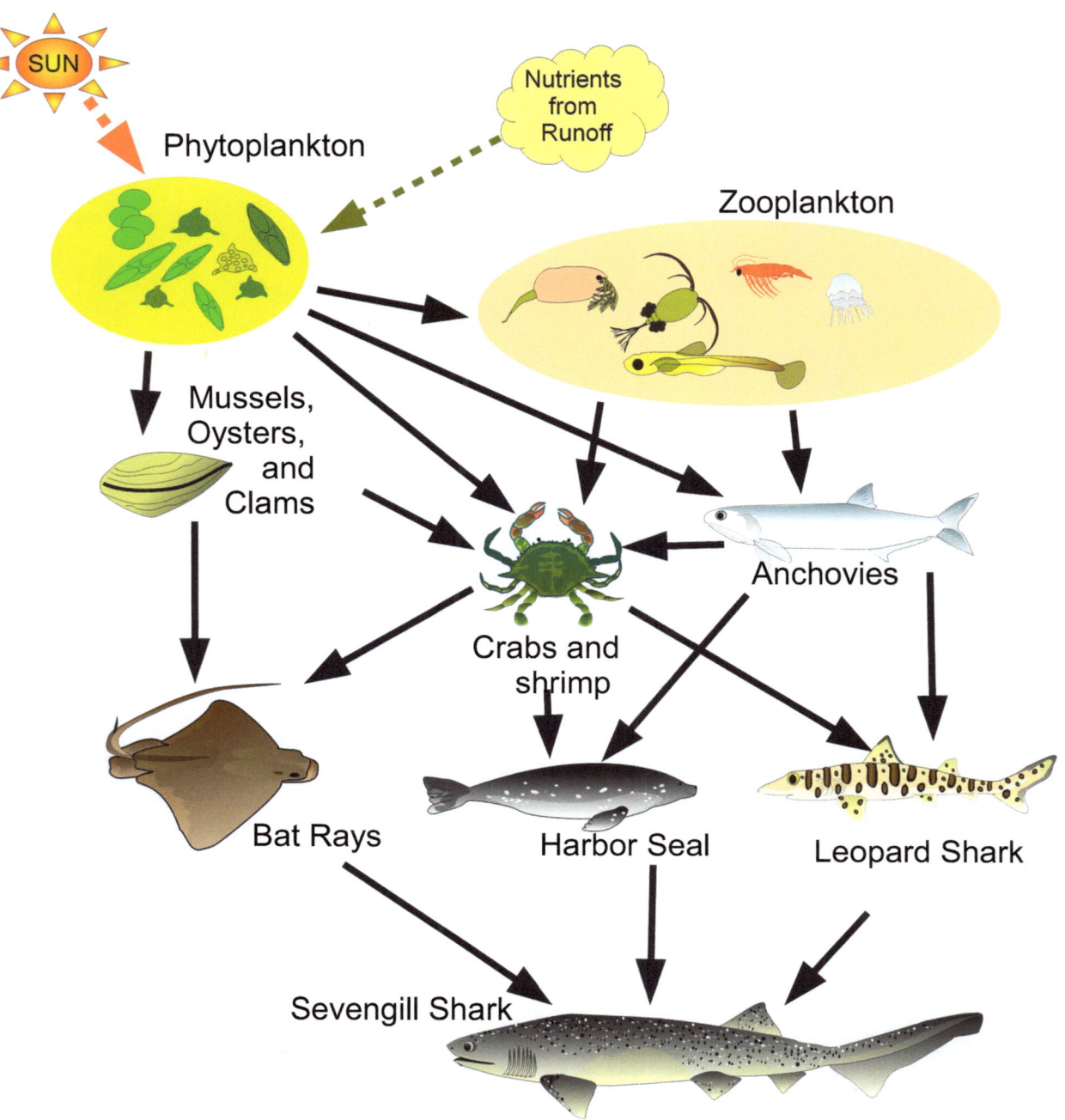

Phytoplankton

SUN

Nutrients from Runoff

Zooplankton

Mussels, Oysters, and Clams

Crabs and shrimp

Anchovies

Bat Rays

Harbor Seal

Leopard Shark

Sevengill Shark

QUESTION:
Sharks are key in the San Francisco Bay ecosystem. If you are a crab and oyster fisher, why should you appreciate sevengill sharks?

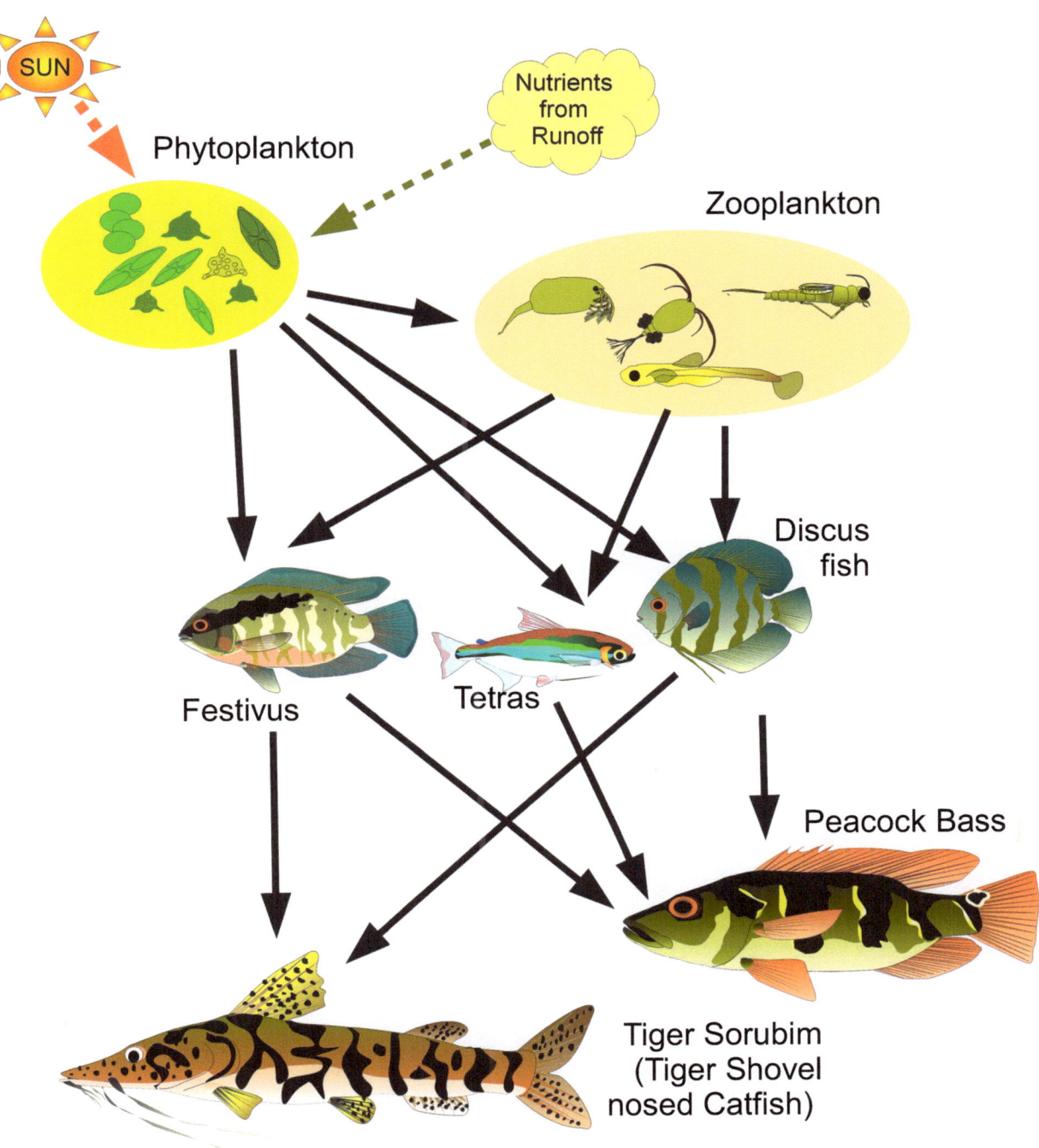

QUESTION:

Why do you think in the Amazon tiger sorubim are sometimes caught on the same fishing lures and in the same spots as peacock bass?

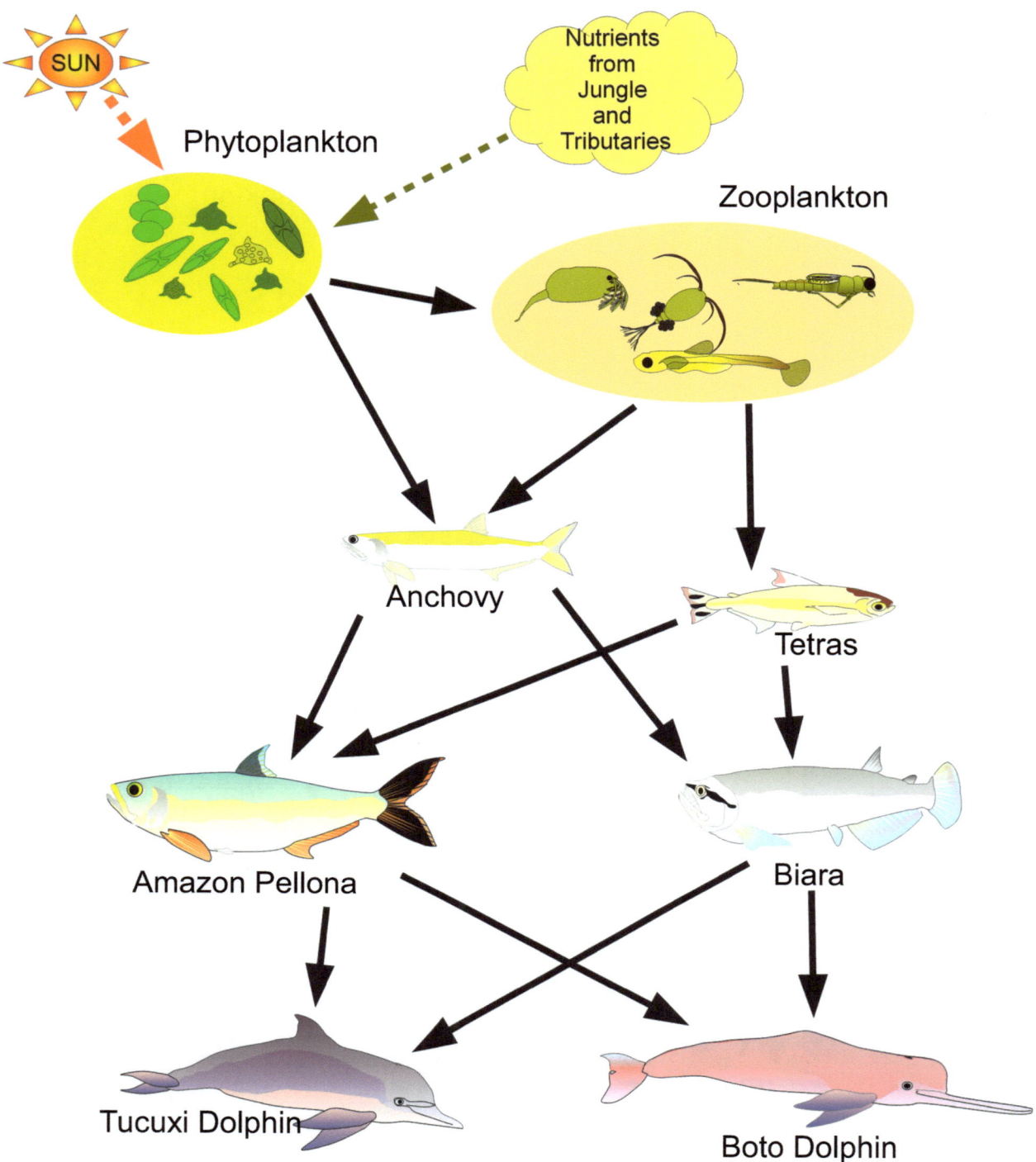

SUN

Phytoplankton

Nutrients from Jungle and Tributaries

Zooplankton

Anchovy

Tetras

Amazon Pellona

Biara

Tucuxi Dolphin

Boto Dolphin

QUESTION:

In the Amazon, anchovies prefer more open water, tetras flooded jungles and thick vegetation. Botos are very good at feeding in flooded jungle, Tucuxi in more open waters. Pelona prefer anchovies. If you see anchovies but few tetras, in open water, which dolphin and predator fish should you also see?

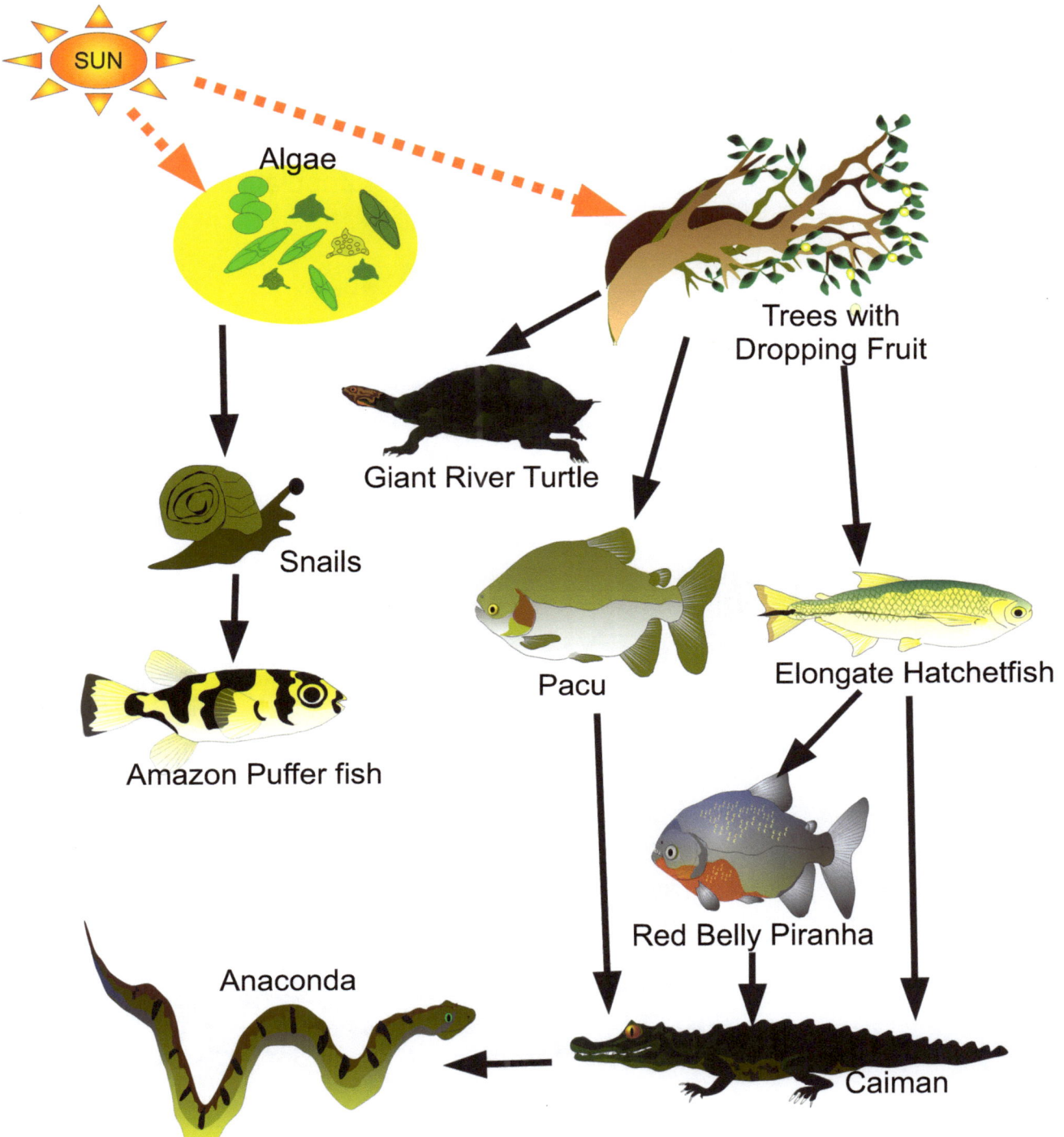

SUN

Algae

Trees with Dropping Fruit

Giant River Turtle

Snails

Amazon Puffer fish

Pacu

Elongate Hatchetfish

Red Belly Piranha

Anaconda

Caiman

QUESTION:

For over a thousand years, fish eating Amazon peoples have tended fruit trees, planting many near flooded riverbanks, even if they don't always eat the fruit. Why do you think they planted these trees? (Clue: Pacu are so tasty, that they are now raised in ponds all over the world.)

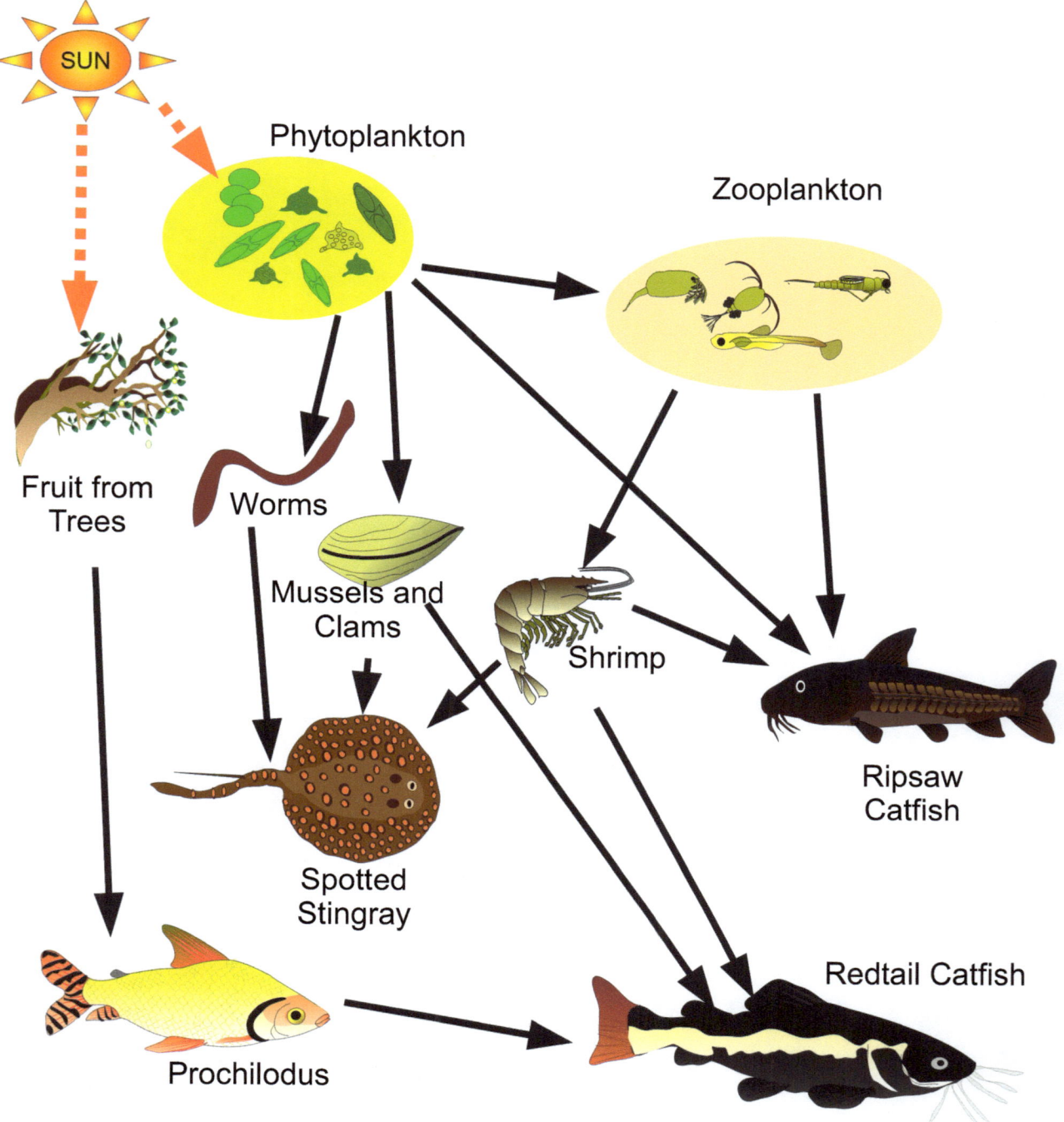

SUN

Phytoplankton

Zooplankton

Fruit from Trees

Worms

Mussels and Clams

Shrimp

Spotted Stingray

Ripsaw Catfish

Prochilodus

Redtail Catfish

QUESTION:

Fruit trees and bushes are good habitat for shrimps, small fishes, insect larvae. What four fishes are also beneficiaries of the trees and bushes, and why for each?

Possible Answers (there are many, these are just mine):

pg. 7: (Indo Pacific Estruaries): They live near river mouths due to the nutrients that feed phytoplankton (and sea grass) that feed the small shrimps they eat.

pg. 8: (Eastern US rivers): Smallies eat mayflies. (In fact they gorge on them in the late spring.)

pg. 9: (Central US) 1) Rainbow and Brown trout compete for the scuds.2)The browns might leave the area, or the growth of both species will slow down. (Side note: Big Browns will eat smaller rainbows too.)

pg. 10: (Central US) The fish population will be very impacted, the fish will loose an insect food source (I have seen it happen).

pg. 11: (FL Keys) Kings eat the same food as sailfish, and will scoop up the wounded ballyhoo missed by the sailfish. Drop a fresh dead ballyhoo under surface in the winter off Islamorada and find out.

pg. 12: (Deep Oceans) The Adult crabs likely die off with the adult tube worms, adult shrimp, and adult clams. However their larvae may drift in the currents to colonize the new hot spot.

pg. 13: (Chesepake Bay) Good populations of Menhaden might clean the water of excess phytoplankton, allowing oxygen to reach oysters, crabs, and fish.

pg. 14: (FL US) Keeping smaller bass allows the tilapia and sunfish populations to grow, in turn allowing the remaining small bass to grow in size.

pg. 15: (Great Lakes) Suckers distract the pike, but also eat the same foods as shiners (which Rock bass eat) and rock bass.

pg. 16: (Southern US) Gulf Kingfish also eat Mole Shrimp, if you see these zipping in the surf, look for the mole shrimp, and hence pompano. Though, since kingfish also eat clams, they might be around when there are no mole shrimp,and no pompano.

pg. 17: (Deep Ocean) They are food for many species, including Anglerfish, Oarfish, Escolar, and Squid. Lantern fish might be one of the most numerous fish in the sea, but we do not know for sure.

pg. 18: (Deep Ocean) Look for Giant Squid and Swordfish!

pg. 19: (CA US) Look for anchovies eating the phytoplankton, though makerel should be eating those, zooplankton eating phytoplankton so sardines, and thresher sharks eating anchovies, mackerel, and sardines.

pg. 20: (FL US) Manatees eat the sea grass, exposing the shrimp for the snappers to eat. Snappers will follow manatees like a cloud.

pg. 21: (Southern US) Crabs would be my first choice, especially near oysters. IF you find crabs and oysters, shrimp are also around. Mullet don't hurt though.

pg. 22: (Tropical Oceans) Leatherback turtles eat jellyfish. Jellyfish eat the things flying fish eat (and eat small flying fish too). More flying fish is better for mahi-mahi. Mahis eat flying fish, marlin eat mahi-mahi.

pg. 23: (Tropical Eastern Pacific) Black Marlin eat small yellowfins since the skipjacks are fewer.

pg. 24: (Antarctica) a) Fewer krill leads to fewer penguins, less food for leopard seals. b) Fewer krill might also lead to fewer Crabeater seals as well, so orcas might target leopard seals more. Side note: recently it was found by scentists that leopard seals eat krill too!

pg. 25: (Open Oceans) Molas eat jellyfish which eat Zooplankton. Sardines eat zooplankton which in turn feed yellowin tuna, birds, and dolphins. Find a patch of zooplankton over an upwell, and you might find tuna.

pg. 26: (Great Lakes) Steelhead eat things (shrimp, large insects) other than alewives. Most of a steelhead's food is not fish. (Note: Large pikes will follow spawning salmon schools.)

pg. 27: (CA US) Great Whites compete with Orcas for seals, so Orcas are eliminating competition.

pg. 28: (CA US and MX) Large Great whites eat sea lions, and will at least scare them enough to keep them close to shore.

pg. 29: (CA US) Mako sharks eat more species then just tuna, especially squids.

pg. 30: (Central US) The Carps eat the same foods as the Shad and Minnows, competeing with the smaller fish. Walleye eat the smaller fish, so fewer smaller fish = fewer walleye. Bigheads also eat shad and minnows, competing directly against the walleye.

pg. 31: (Central US) Large Gars eat the carps, reducing competition for walleye and the walleye's prey.

pg. 32: (Central US) See answer for pg. 30 above. In short, bigheads compete against, and eat shad. Blue Catfish eat shad. Also, bigheads compete against mussels for phytoplankton, blue catfish eat mussels.

pg. 33: (US) Crayfish process carcasses into more crayfish (which are food for catfish and bass), and into nutrients for bacteria-->phytoplanton-->zooplankton-->bluegill.

pg. 34: (CA US) Sevengills eat bat rays, harbor seals, and leopard sharks, which eat crabs (and for rays, oysters).

pg. 35: (Amazon South America) The catfish and peacock bass here eat the same prey fish (Festivus and Discus).

pg. 36: (Amazon South America) Tucuxi Dolphins and Pellona fish.

pg. 37: (Amazon South America) The trees bring in and feed fruit eating fish, including Pacu. Pacu are good for people to eat.

pg. 38: (Amazon South America) Via the shrimp, stingrays, ripsaw catfish (which also benefit from the insects), and redtail catfish. Via the fruit, prochilodus and then redtail catfish. People might eat the shrimp too.

Afterward and Notes:

I made this book for a few reasons:

1) I think even grade school (5th grade and up) children can understand some serious ecology, and it is fun to teach with pictures. The questions force a reader to participate in the learning process. I hope all readers will ask their own questions, and draw their own food webs based upon what they see in the wild. My questions are almost notional.

2) So any angler reading this can catch more fish, or manage their waters.

3) I already drew most of these fish for my (other) children's books. It gave me an excuse to draw more fish too.

I hope you enjoyed using it as much as I enjoyed making it!-
Bryce

If you liked this book you (or the kids) might like my other books including:
•A Fishy, Dolphiny, Squidy, Penguiny, Coloring Book
•Paige's Book of Fishes and Whales
•Grant's Book of Manatees and Dolphins
•Anna's Antarctica
•Lily's Deep Sea Creatures
•Audrey's Amazon River
•(in 2013) Aidyn's California Oceans

  or my website: Http:\\www.combat-fishing.com
•(all the fish herein can be found on clothing etc. there also)